The General Kn

A Complete Co
Knowledge and Pub Quiz Trivia

By Nathan Vurgest

ISBN 9781720348047

First published in 2019

All rights reserved. No part of this book may be reproduced or transmitted by any means without the prior permission of the author.

If you have any comments on any aspect of this book, positive or negative, the author would be very keen to hear from you at Nathan.92@hotmail.co.uk

With thanks to all those who helped, including Vinny, James, Tim, Nicola, Carol and Kate. And I can't forget a special thanks to all those who I have quizzed over the years.

Contents

76) General Knowledge
77) Sport and Leisure
78) General Knowledge
79) Science and Nature
80) General Knowledge
81) The Arts and Entertainment
82) General Knowledge
83) Geography
84) General Knowledge
85) History and politics
86) General Knowledge
87) Sport and Leisure
88) General Knowledge
89) Science and Nature
90) General Knowledge
91) The Arts and Entertainment
92) General Knowledge
93) Geography
94) General Knowledge
95) History and politics
96) General Knowledge
97) Sport and Leisure
98) General Knowledge
99) Science and Nature
100) General Knowledge
101) The Arts and Entertainment
102) General Knowledge
103) Geography
104) General Knowledge
105) History and politics
106) General Knowledge
107) Sport and Leisure
108) General Knowledge
109) Science and Nature
110) General Knowledge
111) The Arts and Entertainment
112) General Knowledge
113) Geography
114) General Knowledge
115) History and politics

116) General Knowledge
117) Sport and Leisure
118) General Knowledge
119) Science and Nature
120) General Knowledge
121) The Arts and Entertainment
122) General Knowledge
123) Geography
124) General Knowledge
125) History and politics
126) General Knowledge
127) Sport and Leisure
128) General Knowledge
129) Science and Nature
130) General Knowledge
131) The Arts and Entertainment
132) General Knowledge
133) Geography
134) General Knowledge
135) History and politics
136) General Knowledge
137) Sport and Leisure
138) General Knowledge
139) Science and Nature
140) General Knowledge
141) The Arts and Entertainment
142) General Knowledge
143) Geography
144) General Knowledge
145) History and politics
146) General Knowledge
147) Sport and Leisure
148) General Knowledge
149) Science and Nature
150) General Knowledge
151) The Arts and Entertainment
152) General knowledge

Introduction

"I have nothing to offer but blood, toil, tears, and sweat" said Winston Churchill in 1940. The phrase came to mind when writing this quiz book and thinking how I can justify the purchasing of it from an author with no prior literary experience or publication track record. This is my first venture into the literary world, but what I do have is a passion for quizzing, an interest in trivia, and a deep seated fascination for world events, which in my opinion is all you need. This has enabled me to share, in this book, what I believe is the most interesting knowledge and fascinating trivia questions, tirelessly researched and created.

I have split this book into general knowledge quizzes, along with specialist quizzes in Geography, History and Politics, Science and Nature, Sport and Leisure, and The Arts and Entertainment, which hopefully will suit any interested quizzer. All questions, I hope, will provide intrigue and amusement, even if some are on the fiendishly difficult side. If you were able to memorise most of the content of this short book, then I believe you would not only have a good grounding for any pub quiz, but a great foundation from which to continue researching into some of the world's most important historical moments, fascinating events, facts and statistics.

I work in economics for my day job, which does to some extent allow me to follow the ups and downs of world events, and around this, my main hobbies are running and hiking, along with travelling and seeing the world. The latter of which has enabled me always to pack a small quiz book with me in my bag wherever I go. Something I hope you all can do with this book. My only other hope is that you enjoy reading it as much as I enjoyed writing it.

Nathan Vurgest

Quiz 1 - Geography

1) 'The Big Easy' is the nickname of which city?

2) The Komodo National Park, famous for its Komodo Dragons, is in which country?

3) Which country has an AK47 rifle on its flag?

4) What is the name of the river running through Paris?

5) Which is the largest city by population in Africa?

6) Which explorer was America named after?

7) Which is the second largest city in Afghanistan, after the capital Kabul?

8) What is the currency of Poland?

9) The main line of the Grand Union canal links which two cities?

10) Cape Horn is in Africa, while the Cape of Good Hope is in South America, true or false?

Quiz 149 – Answers

1) Enid Blyton, 2) Norway, 3) Yann Martel, 4) Billericay and Barry, 5) Freddie 'The Frog' Robdal, 6) Speckled Jim, 7) Moriarty, 8) George Harrison, 9) Argentina, 10) Tom Marvolo Riddle

1) What is Cliff Richard's real name?

2) Which country is the largest producer of oil in the world?

3) What is the term for a person who collaborates with an enemy or is a synonym for a traitor, which originates from the surname of a Norwegian leader?

4) What is 'Davy Jones' locker'?

5) What is the name of the technique most widely used in high jump?

6) Which gift traditionally represents a 40th wedding anniversary?

7) If you are heading 'aft', what are you doing?

8) The author of 'To Kill a Mockingbird', Harper Lee, wrote one other book in her lifetime, what was the name of it?

9) Which region of France has a cabbage named after it?

10) Who was assassinated on the 'Ides of March'?

Quiz 150 – Answers

1) Khrushchev, 2) 46, 3) Caledonia, 4) Pennsylvania Avenue, 5) Spain, 6) True, 7) Cents, 8) Jaws, 9) Nero, 10) Sporty Spice

Quiz 3 - History and Politics

1) The ancient city of Carthage is in which modern day country?

2) Who shot JFK's assassin, Lee Harvey Oswald?

3) Which former UK Prime Minister first famously said "A week is a long time in politics"?

4) Who is said to have drawn a perfect circle for the pope?

5) Which historic leader was nicknamed 'The Scourge of God'?

6) Where in the UK was the Magna Carta signed?

7) What was the name of the 'massacre' in 1819 in Manchester, UK which occurred when cavalry charged at protesters?

8) The Bounty ship's mutineers settled on which group of islands, with direct descendants to this day still making up virtually all its residents?

9) Which King of Sparta was the husband of Helen of Troy?

10) Which war was ended by the treaties of Westphalia?

Quiz 1 – Answers

1) New Orleans, 2) Indonesia, 3) Mozambique, 4) The Seine, 5) Lagos, Nigeria, 6) Amerigo Vespucci, 7) Kandahar, 8) The Polish zloty, 9) Birmingham and London, 10) False, it is the other way round; Cape of Good Hope is in Africa, Cape Horn is in South America

1) If a food has a 'low GI ranking', what does GI stand for?

2) What do you call a person who brings bad luck to a ship?

3) The 'Land of the Rising Sun' refers to which country?

4) Which family live at 742 Evergreen Terrace?

5) Although the Bible doesn't actually mention any number, tradition has it that three wise men visited Jesus. What are their names?

6) Which football club has won the English top division the most times?

7) What is the animal equivalent of the Victoria Cross?

8) What does the 'C' stand for in the famous equation $E=MC^2$?

9) What was the name of the 22 year old White House intern who 49 year old American President Bill Clinton had an affair with?

10) Which actor starred in only one Eon produced James Bond film?

Quiz 2 - Answers

1) Harry Webb, 2) Saudi Arabia, 3) Quisling, 4) The bottom of the sea, 5) Fosbury Flop, 6) Ruby, 7) Moving towards the back of a ship, 8) 'Go Set a Watchman', 9) Savoy, 10) Julius Caesar

1) Toxophily refers to which sport?

2) Which French football team plays at the Stade Louis II stadium?

3) In which sport is the Stanley Cup contested?

4) Which American race is the world's oldest annual marathon?

5) Which shirt number is usually worn by a fullback in rugby union?

6) At which Grand Prix was Ayrton Senna killed?

7) Who coached the GB men's football team at the 2012 London Olympics?

8) In English cricket, which county have won the county championship the most times?

9) In which U.S state is the Green Bay Packers American Football team based?

10) Which international football team shares its nickname with Manchester United?

Quiz 3 – Answers

1) Tunisia, 2) Jack Ruby, 3) Harold Wilson, 4) Giotto, 5) Attila the Hun, 6) Runnymede, 7) Peterloo Massacre, 8) The Pitcairn islands, 9) King Menalaus, 10) Thirty years war

1) Magyar is the official language of which country?

2) Which country donates a Christmas tree, displayed in Trafalgar Square, London, to the people of Britain every year, as a token of gratitude for support during the Second World War?

3) Who flew too close to the sun in Greek mythology?

4) Over which course is the Scottish Grand National run?

5) In which county is Sandringham House, the private home of the Queen?

6) In which country was the last recorded sighting of the dodo?

7) Who provided the voice for Woody in the film Toy Story?

8) The Toronto Blue Jays play which sport?

9) What is the Roman numeral for 50?

10) The E street Band is which famous artist's backing band?

Quiz 4 – Answers

1) Glycaemic Index, 2) A Jonah, 3) Japan, 4) The Simpsons, 5) Caspar, Balthasar, and Melchior, 6) Manchester United, 7) Dicken Medal, 8) Speed of light, 9) Monica Lewinsky, 10) George Lazenby ('On Her Majesty's Secret Service')

1) Which is the only bird that can fly backwards?

2) To the nearest whole number, how many Kilograms in a stone?

3) How is the day that is the start of the shooting season for Red Grouse in Britain more commonly known?

4) Who is widely accredited with first discovering oxygen?

5) What do the computer initials URL stand for?

6) In which city are the headquarters of the UK Met office?

7) Which element is also known as quicksilver?

8) What is a leveret?

9) What do the initials SIM, the card used in mobile phones, stand for?

10) At what temperature are degrees Fahrenheit and degrees Celsius the same?

Quiz 5 – Answers

1) Archery, 2) AS Monaco, 3) Ice Hockey, 4) Boston Marathon, 5) 15, 6) San Marino Grand Prix in Imola, Italy, 7) Stuart Pearce, 8) Yorkshire, 9) Wisconsin, 10) Belgium (The Red Devils)

1) What is the currency of Thailand?

2) Abbey Road, made famous by the Beatles, is in which city?

3) What was the name of the Greenpeace boat, which was sunk in the port of Auckland, New Zealand, by the French Intelligence Service?

4) Canada's national dish 'Poutine' consists of which three main ingredients?

5) How long in yards is a cricket pitch?

6) What was the name of the mission that landed the first man on the moon?

7) Which male name is used in radio transmission to signify 'received and understood'?

8) Olive Oyl is the girlfriend of which cartoon character?

9) The Berlin wall was taken down in 1989, but what year was it erected?

10) Which sculptor created the Angel of the North?

Quiz 6 – Answers

1) Hungary, 2) Norway, 3) Icarus, 4) Ayr Racecourse, 5) Norfolk, 6) Mauritius, 7) Tom Hanks, 8) Baseball, 9) L, 10) Bruce Springsteen

Quiz 9 - The Arts and Entertainment

1) Which artist painted 'The Laughing Cavalier'?

2) What is the stage name of the lead guitarist of U2?

3) Which economist wrote 'The Wealth of Nations'?

4) Spock, the First Officer of the Starship Enterprise in Star Trek, is from which planet?

5) With which cartoon series would you associate `The Buzzwagon`, `The Crimson Haybayler` and `The Mean Machine`?

6) Which actor plays Marty McFly in the 'Back to The Future' series of movies?

7) What is 'J.K.' short for with regard to the author J.K. Rowling?

8) Which book came first in the novel series, Fifty Shades Darker or Fifty Shades Freed?

9) Who wrote the renowned novel 'A Passage to India'?

10) What is Kate's name short for in series two of Blackadder?

Quiz 7 – Answers

1) Hummingbird, 2) 6, 3) The glorious 12th, 4) Joseph Priestly, 5) Uniform Resource Locator, 6) Exeter, 7) Mercury, 8) A young hare, 9) Subscriber Identity Module, 10) -40

1) What is the name of the famous bronze sculpture in Brussels of a boy urinating into a fountain basin?

2) According to legend, Lady Godiva rode naked through which city's streets?

3) The band Blink 182 gets its name from the number of times Al Pacino uses the `f word` in which film?

4) To the nearest 10%, what per cent of the world's population lives in the Southern Hemisphere?

5) In 1919, which two people completed the first non-stop transatlantic flight?

6) What is "Tiger" Woods first name?

7) According to the Bible, what is God said to have created on the fourth day of creation?

8) What is the most expensive man-made object ever built?

9) What do the initials QC stand for after a Barristers name?

10) How many keys are there on a standard piano?

Quiz 8 – Answers

1) The Thai baht, 2) London, 3) The Rainbow Warrior, 4) Chips, gravy, cheese curds, 5) 22 yards, 6) Apollo 11, 7) Roger, 8) Popeye, 9) 1961, 10) Antony Gormley

12

1) Which country is the largest producer of tea in the world?

2) Who was the first European to discover New Zealand? Clue: It wasn't James Cook.

3) Located mostly in California and Nevada, what is the driest desert in North America? This Desert is also home to 'Death Valley'.

4) Hispaniola is the island shared by which two countries?

5) The Great Bear Lake is in which country?

6) Which hills form part of the border between England and Scotland?

7) Mount Chimborazo in Ecuador is known for being what?

8) What is the capital of the state of Utah?

9) What is the name of the grassland and fertile plains that span Uruguay, Argentina and Brazil?

10) The Murray River is the longest river in which country?

Quiz 9 – Answers

1) Frans Hals, 2) The Edge, 3) Adam Smith, 4) Vulcan, 5) Wacky Races, 6) Michael J Fox, 7) Joanne Kathleen, 8) Fifty Shades Darker,9) E. M. Forster, 10) Bob

Quiz 12 - General Knowledge

1) The dog 'Nipper' features on the logo of which famous chain of entertainment stores?

2) What are the four time zones of mainland USA?

3) Montego Bay is a holiday resort on which island?

4) Which country is Singha beer from?

5) Who was the first ever prime minister of Great Britain?

6) The Oval in London is the home of which county cricket team?

7) Which berries are used in the making of gin?

8) What colour is a polar bear's skin?

9) Quasimodo is a fictional character from which novel?

10) Which snooker player is known as 'The Rocket'?

Quiz 10 – Answers

1) Mannekin Pis, 2) Coventry,3) Scarface, 4) 10%, 5) Alcock and Brown, 6) Eldrick, 7) The stars and heavenly bodies, 8) The International Space Station, 9) Queen's Council, 10) 88

1) HMS Victory was a ship best known to be used in which famous battle?

2) The Chappaquiddick incident involved which famous person, supposedly causing him to abandon his potential political career?

3) The Battle of the Alamo was between which two opposing sides?

4) The 'Gang of Four' led to the formation of what in the UK?

5) In which modern day country was Mother Teresa born?

6) What were followers of Oliver Cromwell known as?

7) Who did John Hinckley Jr. wound in an assassination attempt?

8) What were the occupations of the 'Cambridge Five'?

9) What is the name of the airport in Uganda where 45 Ugandan soldiers and 7 hijackers were killed in a hostage rescue mission by Israeli Soldiers in 1976?

10) The Zimmermann telegram proposed a military alliance between Germany and which country?

Quiz 11 – Answers

1) China, 2) Abel Tasman, 3) The Mojave Desert, 4) Haiti and Dominican Republic, 5) Canada, 6) Cheviot Hills, 7) The closest point on earth to outer space, i.e. even closer than Mount Everest!, 8) Salt Lake City, 9) The Pampas, 10) Australia

1) What is the name of Mickey Mouse's dog?

2) The M11 motorway goes from London to which city?

3) Fill in the missing US president: Carter, [.....], Bush, Clinton.

4) What is the UK area telephone dialling code for Birmingham?

5) The 'Flop', 'River', and 'Turn' appear in which game?

6) What colour is caffeine?

7) Which country has the largest population of wild camels in the world?

8) Which country gifted the Statue of Liberty to the U.S.A as a commemoration of independence?

9) Who played Frodo Baggins in the Lord of the Rings films?

10) In road cycling racing, there are three Grand Tours; the Tour De France, Giro d'Italia and which other?

Quiz 12 – Answers

1) HMV, 2) Eastern, Central, Mountain, and Pacific, 3) Jamaica, 4) Thailand, 5) Robert Walpole, 6) Surrey, 7) Juniper berries, 8) Black, 9) The Hunchback of Notre-Dame, 10) Ronnie O'Sullivan

Quiz 15 - Sport and Leisure

1) Which chess computer built by IBM defeated world chess champion Garry Kasparov?

2) Who is nicknamed 'The Golden Bear' in Golf?

3) From which country did the Rubik's cube originate?

4) In 2009, Jenson Button won the Formula 1 World Drivers' Championship with which team?

5) In which country did the "Rumble in The Jungle" take place?

6) What does a fletcher do?

7) How many players are there in a baseball team?

8) Which female athlete won gold for Great Britain in the 2012 Olympic Games Heptathlon event?

9) Which Colombian Goalkeeper made a name for himself by performing a 'Scorpion kick' during a football match against England?

10) What major sporting event takes place at Churchill Downs every year?

Quiz 13 – Answers

1) Battle of Trafalgar, 2) Edward Kennedy, 3) Mexico and Texas, 4) The Social Democrat Party (SDP), 5) North Macedonia, 6) The Roundheads, 7) Ronald Regan, 8) Spies/Intelligence officers (they were all double agents for the USSR), 9) Entebbe, 10) Mexico

1) What is the most southern point of mainland UK?

2) What was the Roman name for Ireland?

3) Who is said to have cut the Gordian knot?

4) Complete the set; The Angel Islington, Euston Road...?

5) Before Andy Murray, who was the last British male tennis player to win Wimbledon?

6) Which single ingredient is the difference between a Martini and a Dirty Martini?

7) What do you call a group of parrots?

8) The drummer for the band Nirvana, after its collapse, went on to be the lead singer of which band?

9) What are the first three words of the King James Bible?

10) Timbuktu is a city in which country?

Quiz 14 – Answers

1) Pluto, 2) Cambridge, 3) Reagan, 4) 0121, 5) Texas Hold 'Em Poker, 6) White, 7) Australia, 8) France, 9) Elijah Wood, 10) Vuelta a España

1) What does the term 'AIDS' stand for?

2) What is the most abundant metal in the earth's crust?

3) Which fruit is also known as a love apple?

4) Which is a longer period of time, an epoch or a period?

5) What does the English car brand MG's name stand for?

6) What do you call the home of a squirrel?

7) What does the Mohs scale measure?

8) Vitamin B2 is also known as what?

9) Who completed the first ever human heart transplant?

10) What was the name of the C-shaped supercontinent that existed during the late Palaeozoic and early Mesozoic era before it broke apart eventually forming the continents we know today?

Quiz 15 – Answers

1) Deep Blue, 2) Jack Nicklaus, 3) Hungary, 4) Brawn GP, 5) Zaire, now known as the Democratic Republic of Congo, 6) Makes and sells arrows, 7) 9, 8) Jessica Ennis, 9) Rene Higuita, 10) The Kentucky Derby

1) As of 2020, which is the busiest airport in the world by number of passengers?

2) Which island was awarded the George Cross during World War II?

3) Who was the first person to reach the summit of Mount Everest and return safely?

4) What was the name of the athlete who competed for Great Britain at the 1984 Olympics and who is famous for usually running barefoot?

5) Which capital city is located closest to the equator?

6) What vegetable is often used in the production of vodka?

7) What is the breed of dog often nicknamed a 'sausage dog'?

8) What was Victoria Beckham's surname before she married?

9) What is the international telephone dialling code for the USA?

10) What was Muhammad Ali's birth name?

Quiz 16 – Answers

1) Lizard Point, 2) Hibernia, 3) Alexander the Great, 4) Pentonville Road (the blue set on a Monopoly board), 5) Fred Perry, 6) Olive Juice, 7) A Pandemonium, 8) Foo Fighters (David Grohl), 9) In the Beginning, 10) Mali

1) Wisteria Lane features in which fictional TV show?

2) Named after a Mongol ruler and Chinese emperor, what is the name of the famous poem by Samuel Taylor Coleridge?

3) Where was Rihanna born?

4) What is the name of the sitcom written by Ben Elton and starring Rowan Atkinson which focuses on a police station in the fictional town of Gasforth?

5) "You're gonna need a bigger boat" is a famous line from which film?

6) Who wrote Tess of the d'Urbervilles?

7) Which fictional character is Edgar Rice Burroughs famous for creating?

8) What is the name of Sarah Jessica Parker's character in the TV series `Sex and the city`?

9) In which fictional book series is there a currency made up of bronze Knuts, silver Sickles and golden Galleons?

10) Who composed the orchestral suite 'The Planets'?

Quiz 17 – Answers

1) Acquired immune deficiency syndrome, 2) Aluminium, 3) A tomato, 4) A period, 5) Morris Garages, 6) A dray, 7) Mineral hardness, 8) Riboflavin, 9) Christian Barnard, 10) Pangea

1) Also the name of a type of helicopter, what is the term for a wind travelling through the Canadian Prairies and Rocky mountain range in North America?

2) In Roman mythology who was the Goddess of the moon?

3) What is the name of the former heavyweight champion boxer who has also served as the Mayor of Kiev?

4) What do you call a group of camels?

5) 'To be or not to be' is a phrase from which Shakespeare play?

6) What does SCUBA stand for in SCUBA Diving?

7) Which suffragette stepped in front of the King's horse at the 1913 Epsom Derby and subsequently died from her injuries?

8) What famous nickname is given to an area within Santa Clara County?

9) What type of animal was Speedy Gonzales?

10) From which language does the word Yoghurt come from?

Quiz 18 – Answers

1) Hartsfield-Jackson Atlanta airport, 2) Malta, 3) Edmund Hillary, 4) Zola Budd, 5) Quito, Ecuador, 6) Potato, 7) Dachshund, 8) Adams, 9) +1 or 001, 10) Cassius Clay

1) St Peter Port is the capital of which British island?

2) Which river forms most of the border between Mexico and the USA?

3) What is the name of the only Cape in England?

4) In which country is the highest waterfall in Europe?

5) The city of Milwaukee is in which U.S state?

6) Which 'sea' is actually the largest lake in the world?

7) Which hills are also known as 'the backbone of Italy'?

8) What is the former name of New York City?

9) What is the national religion of Japan?

10) The Palk Strait is between which two countries?

Quiz 19 – Answers

1) Desperate Housewives, 2) Kubla Khan, 3) Barbados, 4) The Thin Blue Line, 5) Jaws, 6) Thomas Hardy, 7) Tarzan, 8) Carrie (Bradshaw), 9) The Harry Potter series, 10) Gustav Holst

1) Famous for the brand name of pies, in which country is the city of Fray Bentos?

2) Which famous battle was fought on Senlac Hill?

3) The Los Angeles Lakers play which sport?

4) How many bits in a byte?

5) Which country's cars have the international vehicle registration code of the letter 'D'?

6) In the `Dukes Of Hazzard` what was the name of Duke's car?

7) Denali is the tallest mountain in which country?

8) Who was known as 'Il Duce'?

9) Which athlete is nicknamed 'The Lightning Bolt'?

10) Which famous musician narrated the adventures of Thomas the Tank Engine on British television?

Quiz 20 – Answers

1) Chinook, 2) Luna, 3) Vitali Klitschko, 4) A caravan, 5) Hamlet, 6) Self-contained underwater breathing apparatus, 7) Emily Davison, 8) Silicon Valley, 9) A mouse, 10) Turkish

1) In what year was the Gunpowder Plot?

2) Who found Tutankhamun's tomb?

3) Who led the first successful expedition to reach the South Pole?

4) Who invented the 'Bouncing Bomb'?

5) In which country was the Hyphen war?

6) Who was nicknamed 'Old blood and guts'?

7) What is the former Asian country of Siam now known as?

8) Who was the last UK governor of Hong Kong?

9) Which company owned the RMS Titanic?

10) What was the former currency of the Netherlands before it joined the Euro?

Quiz 21 – Answers

1) Guernsey, 2) Rio Grande, 3) Cape Cornwall, 4) Norway, 5) Wisconsin, 6) Caspian Sea, 7) The Apennine Range, 8) New Amsterdam, 9) Shinto, 10) Sri Lanka and India

1) What is the name of the town in Coronation Street?

2) Warsaw has the largest Polish population in the world, but which city in America has the second largest?

3) What is the name of the art of reading people's palms called?

4) What rice is typically used to make risotto?

5) Axl Rose is the lead singer of which Rock Band?

6) Which country had a referendum in 1999 to decide whether to retain the British Monarchy or become a republic?

7) Which one of the following is not a decathlon event? Shot Putt, 400 meters, Triple Jump, Long Jump, High Jump?

8) Conkers come from which type of tree?

9) What was the name of Ian Fleming's home and estate on the Island of Jamaica, which is also the name of a James Bond film?

10) Which hand scores higher in poker, a flush or straight?

Quiz 22 – Answers

1) Uruguay, 2) Battle of Hastings, 3) Basketball, 4) 8, 5) Germany, 6) General Lee, 7) The USA (it used to be known as Mount McKinley), 8) Benito Mussolini, 9) Usain Bolt, 10) Ringo Starr

1) In which country was Snooker invented by a member of the British Army?

2) In the 2006 World Cup Final, Zinedine Zidane was sent off for head-butting which Italian player?

3) What is the maximum number of clubs a golfer is allowed to carry in a match?

4) What colour is Coventry Street on a standard monopoly board?

5) What is the name of the Formula 1 driver who died in 2015 after sustaining injuries in a crash at the Japanese Grand Prix in 2014?

6) Who won the first Rugby Union World Cup?

7) The 'Thrilla in Manilla' was the third and final boxing match between Muhammed Ali and whom?

8) Which British World's Strongest Man competition winner also competed in the Olympics in the 1970s and 80's in the Shot Putt event?

9) Who scored the first ever Premier League goal?

10) The Buffalo Bills play which sport?

Quiz 23 – Answers

1) 1605, 2) Howard Carter, 3) Roald Amundsen, 4) Barnes Wallace, 5) Czechoslovakia, 6) General George Patton, 7) Thailand, 8) Chris Patten, 9) White Star Line, 10) Dutch guilder

1) What is traditionally used to encase the ingredients of haggis?

2) Rome was built on how many hills?

3) Albert Einstein was offered the presidency of which country, but turned it down?

4) How many times bigger than a normal wine bottle is a Nebuchadnezzar?

5) What shape is the DNA molecule?

6) What are there said to be none of in Ireland, as St Patrick reputedly banished them from the land?

7) In which country was the actor Russell Crowe born?

8) Who married Adolph Hitler shortly before they both committed suicide?

9) Who managed Blackburn Rovers when they won the English Premier League in 1995?

10) With what two words do the names of the episodes of the TV show `Friends` usually begin with?

Quiz 24 – Answers

1) Weatherfield, 2) Chicago, 3) Palmistry, 4) Arborio rice, 5) Guns 'N' Roses, 6) Australia, 7) Triple Jump, 8) Horse Chestnut tree, 9) Goldeneye, 10) Flush

Quiz 27 - Science and Nature

1) Which planet of the solar system has its 27 moons named after characters from the works of William Shakespeare and Alexander Pope?

2) Which extant bird has the widest wingspan?

3) In physics, what is the 'God Particle' also known as?

4) What is the term for a glacial valley or trough found along the coast that is filled with a mixture of fresh water and sea water?

5) What is the boiling temperature of water in Fahrenheit?

6) What is the name of a triangle with three unequal sides?

7) What is the atomic number of Oxygen?

8) What was the name of the first artificial satellite put into space?

9) In what year did Halley's Comet last appear in the inner parts of the solar system, visible from earth by the human eye?

10) What type of animal is a glow worm? Hint: it's not a worm

---

Quiz 25 – Answers

1) India, 2) Marco Materazzi, 3) 14, 4) Yellow, 5) Jules Bianchi, 6) New Zealand, 7) Joe Frazier, 8) Geoff Capes, 9) Brian Deane, 10) American Football

1) What is the nickname of the state of New York?

2) Who was King Arthur's wife in folklore?

3) The cocktail Kir Royal consists of which two ingredients?

4) Who still holds the Triple Jump world record, despite setting it back in 1995?

5) In radio terminology what does FM stand for?

6) What are the names of the four mutant ninja turtles?

7) Newton Heath was the former name of which football club?

8) The Spanish steps are a famous tourist attraction in which city?

9) What do the initials AD stand for in the calendar and what do they translate as?

10) Which sitcom is set in Walmington-On-sea?

Quiz 26 – Answers

1) A sheep's stomach, 2) 7, 3) Israel, 4) 20, 5) Double Helix, 6) Snakes, 7) New Zealand, 8) Eva Braun, 9) Kenny Dalglish, 10) `The one...`

Quiz 29 - The Arts and Entertainment

1) What is the name of Bart Simpson`s dog?

2) What is the name of the sequel to the film 'Saturday Night Fever'?

3) Marc Bolan, who died in a car crash aged 29, was the lead singer of which band?

4) Name the five Thunderbird brothers?

5) What exactly is 'Skyfall' in the James Bond Movie?

6) Which three characters accompany Dorothy to find the Wizard of Oz?

7) "Wax on, wax off" is a phrase in which 1984 film?

8) What do the initials BAFTA stand for?

9) What is the name of Tom Cruise`s character in the film `Mission Impossible`?

10) In what year was 'The day the music died"?

Quiz 27 – Answers

1) Uranus, 2) The wandering albatross, 3) The Higgs boson, 4) A Fjord, 5) 212, 6) A scalene triangle, 7) 8, 8) Sputnik, 9) 1986, 10) A Beetle

1) The city of Kathmandu is in which country?

2) Which Roman Emperor supposedly made his horse a senator?

3) Which football team does Prince William support?

4) What are the three ingredients of a Margarita cocktail?

5) What is the name for someone who puts shoes on horses' hooves?

6) What does the W stand for in George W Bush?

7) In the Lion King, where do Mufasa and his family live?

8) What is the name of the famous park in Dublin, which is one of the largest parks in Europe?

9) Georgi Markov was assassinated on Waterloo Bridge in London by someone wielding what implement?

10) Who painted 'The Scream'?

Quiz 28 – Answers

1) The Empire state, 2) Guinevere, 3) Crème de Casis and Champagne, 4) Jonathon Edwards, 5) Frequency modulation, 6) Leonardo, Donatello, Michelangelo, Raphael, 7) Manchester United, 8) Rome, Italy, 9) Anno Domini, meaning 'in the year of the Lord', 10) Dad's Army

1) What is the tallest mountain in New Zealand?

2) Also famous for its variety of wildlife, what is the name of the distinctive body of water bounded by four currents which forms a region of the Atlantic Ocean, yet unlike all other seas, borders no countries?

3) Which lake on the river Nile is the third largest reservoir in the world?

4) What is the county town of Kent?

5) Where are the highest sea cliffs in the world?

6) What is the name of the UK islet in the north Atlantic, off the coast of the Outer Hebrides, which also shares its name with a shipping forecast area?

7) Which is closer to Spain, the Spanish Steps or the Spanish Riding School?

8) Which is the longest river in Scotland?

9) Southern Rhodesia is the former name of which modern day country?

10) What is the capital city of Pakistan?

Quiz 29 – Answers

1) Santa`s Little Helper, 2) 'Staying Alive', 3) T. Rex., 4) Scott, John, Virgil, Gordon, Alan, 5) The Bond Family home, 6) Scarecrow, Tin Woodman, and the Cowardly Lion, 7) The Karate Kid, 8) British Academy of Film and Television Arts, 9) Ethan Hunt, 10) 1959

1) Who was the driver of the car that Diana, Princess of Wales was travelling in when it crashed, resulting in her death?

2) Which athlete has won the most Olympic medals?

3) From which modern day country does Pilsner beer come from?

4) What does the phrase 'Veni vidi vici' mean?

5) How many Kings did England have in the year of 1066?

6) What do you call a castrated male horse?

7) Which two countries are at either ends of the 'Rainbow Bridge'?

8) What was the nickname of the dinosaur which took centre stage in the entrance of the Natural History Museum in London for 112 years until it was relocated in 2016?

9) What is the newest country in the world as of 2020?

10) Who said the now famous quote "In the future, everyone will be world-famous for 15 minutes"?

Quiz 30 – Answers

1) Nepal, 2) Caligula, 3) Aston Villa, 4) Tequila, Triple sec, Lime Juice, 5) Farrier, 6) Walker, 7) Pride Rock, 8) Phoenix Park, 9) A poison-tipped Umbrella, 10) Edvard Munch

1) Who was the Argentinian ruler at the start of the Falklands War?

2) Said to be one of the most important inventions ever, what did Johannes Gutenberg invent?

3) The codename for the combat phase of the 1990-1991 Gulf War was 'Operation...'?

4) Who was the last British monarch to be killed in battle, and was slain in the battle of Flodden?

5) Which two countries fought in the War of Jenkins's Ear in the 18th century?

6) What was the name of the Swedish Prime Minister who was assassinated in 1986 in what remains an unsolved crime?

7) Which Roman road ran from London to York?

8) Who was the youngest ever British Prime Minister?

9) Which king ordered the creation of the Doomsday book?

10) Which squadron number were the 'Dam Busters' from?

Quiz 31 – Answers

1) Mt Cook, 2) Sargasso Sea, 3) Lake Nasser, 4) Maidstone, 5) Hawaii, 6) Rockall, 7) The Spanish steps. The Spanish steps are a famous tourist attraction in Rome, Italy, and the Spanish Riding School is a famous traditional riding school in Vienna, Austria. 8) River Tay, 9) Zimbabwe, 10) Islamabad

1) What is the former name of the city of Beijing?

2) Annually, what is the most visited country in the world from a tourism perspective?

3) Hannibal was a general of which empire?

4) Which snooker player has won the World Championship the most times with seven wins?

5) How many people have ever walked on the moon?

6) What is 'oeuf' in France?

7) What is the name of Elton John's husband?

8) The Battle of Agincourt was a major English victory in which war?

9) What is the name for the form of clarified butter that is commonly used in South Asian cuisines?

10) What is Mr Darcy's first name in Pride and Prejudice?

Quiz 32 – Answers

1) Henri Paul, 2) Michael Phelps, 3) Czech Republic, 4) I came, I saw, I conquered, 5) Three; Edward the Confessor, Harold Godwinson, William the Conqueror (Edgar Etheling was elected, but never actually crowned King), 6) A gelding, 7) USA and Canada (it's at the Niagara Falls), 8) Dippy, 9) South Sudan, 10) Andy Warhol

Quiz 35 - Sport and Leisure

1) Of which state is Dog Mushing the official state sport?

2) Which track and field event did Steve Backley compete in, an event in which he still holds the British record in?

3) Which recently retired cricket commentator is known as 'Blowers'?

4) Which country's rugby team are nicknamed 'The Pumas'?

5) Which team won the last ever football first division in England before the formation of the Premier League the following season?

6) In darts, what is it called when you hit a single, double, and triple of the same number?

7) Who became both the youngest and oldest player to win the Golf Masters, in 1963 and 1986?

8) From 1999 to 2017 a Formula 1 Grand Prix took place at the Sepang International Circuit, but in which country is this circuit?

9) How many consecutive touches can a volleyball team make before the ball has to be passed over the net?

10) Which Spanish football team plays at the Mestalla Stadium?

Quiz 33 – Answers

1) General Galtieri, 2) The printing press, 3) Desert Storm, 4) James IV of Scotland, 5) England and Spain, 6) Olof Palme, 7) Ermine Street, 8) William Pitt the Younger, 9) William the Conqueror, 10) 617 squadron

1) Canary Wharf is on which London underground line?

2) Whose face featured on the First World War recruitment posters often with the exclamation that "Your country needs you"?

3) Who was Team GB's flag bearer in the opening ceremony at the London 2012 Olympics?

4) What is the name of Rod Stewart's famous band?

5) What transforms a gin into a pink gin?

6) 'Houston, we have a problem' is a phrase associated with which Space mission?

7) What was the composer Mozart's first name?

8) The 'Cod wars' were a fishing dispute between which two countries?

9) Which river runs through the Grand Canyon?

10) In which English city is the film `The Full Monty` set?

Quiz 34 – Answers

1) Peking, 2) France, 3) Carthage, 4) Stephen Hendry, 5) Twelve, 6) Egg, 7) David Furnish, 8) The Hundred Years War, 9) Ghee, 10) Fitzwilliam

Quiz 37 - Science and Nature

1) What do the computer initials HTML stand for?

2) What is the name of Saturn's largest moon?

3) Strange, charm, up, down, top, and bottom are types of what?

4) What is the largest fish in the world?

5) Who is known as "The father of medicine"?

6) What is H5N1 more commonly known as?

7) Who invented the diesel engine?

8) What was the name of the man who broke eight world speed records on water and on land in the 1950s and 1960s and died during a water speed record attempt at Coniston Water? His body was eventually recovered in 2001.

9) What does PVC stand for?

10) What is 'Hale-Bopp'?

Quiz 35 – Answers

1) Alaska, 2) Javelin, 3) Henry Blofeld, 4) Argentina, 5) Leeds United, 6) Shanghai, 7) Jack Nicklaus, 8) Malaysia, 9) Three, 10) Valencia

1) St Helier is a parish situated on which island?

2) Prior to 2012, in which year did London last host the Olympic Games?

3) Although not proven, which city is believed by historians to have been the first city to have over one million inhabitants?

4) Who invented the World Wide Web, while working at CERN?

5) Which sign of the zodiac is symbolized by a ram?

6) In which city is the film Trainspotting set?

7) Which famous sauce is made on Avery Island, Louisiana?

8) Who captained the English football team in the 1966 World Cup final?

9) Which two countries fought in the Hundred Years' War?

10) Table Mountain is in which country?

Quiz 36 – Answers

1) Jubilee line, 2) Lord Kitchener, 3) Sir Chris Hoy, 4) The Faces, 5) Angostura bitters, 6) Apollo 13, 7) Wolfgang, 8) The UK and Iceland, 8) Colorado River, 9) Sheffield

Quiz 39 - The Arts and Entertainment

1) Whose most famous catchphrases are "it's a cracker!" and "It's the way I tell 'em!"

2) Who was the host of the BBC sports quiz show 'Question of Sport' from 1979 to 1997, prior to being replaced by Sue Barker?

3) Who designed Catherine Middleton's wedding dress?

4) What art movement/style is associated with Vincent Van Gogh?

5) What are Avada Kedavra, Crucio and Imperio in the Harry Potter books?

6) Which superhero has his body enhanced by an injection of a special serum during WWII?

7) In the film 'Speed', the bus cannot go below what speed?

8) Who is Princess Leia's twin?

9) Who was the American jazz clarinettist who was known as the 'King of Swing'?

10) What is the name of Cassandra's father and Rodney's father in law in Only Fools and Horses?

Quiz 37 – Answers

1) Hypertext Markup Language, 2) Titan, 3) Quarks, 4) The whale shark, 5) Hippocrates, 6) Bird flu/Avian influenza, 7) Rudolph Diesel, 8) Donald Campbell, 9) Polyvinyl chloride, 10) A comet

1) What type of pastry is used in profiteroles?

2) What was the former currency of Portugal before it joined the Euro?

3) In which Disney movie is there a monkey named Abu?

4) Which soldier and politician was known as the 'King of the wild frontier'?

5) Which London football club was the first in England to install an artificial pitch?

6) Which British peerage is between Baron and Earl?

7) What does the 'E' stand for in the food additives 'E numbers'?

8) In which U.S state is Las Vegas?

9) What is the phonetic alphabet word for 'J'?

10) What is the name of the Spanish town bombed in the Spanish Civil War, which is also the name of a painting by Pablo Picasso depicting the event?

Quiz 38 – Answers

1) Jersey, 2) 1948, 3) Rome, 4) Tim Berners Lee, 5) Aries, 6) Edinburgh, 7) Tabasco Sauce, 8) Bobby Moore, 9) England and France, 10) South Africa

Quiz 41 - Geography

1) What is the county town of Derbyshire?

2) Guadalcanal, a famous World War II battle site, is the largest island of which island group?

3) Which country is the largest producer of cocoa in the world?

4) What is the biggest and busiest (by cargo tonnage) port in Europe?

5) Which river runs from the Great Lakes to the Atlantic Ocean, passing through Montreal?

6) What is the name of the 1250km long Russian peninsula lying between the Pacific Ocean and the Sea of Okhotsk?

7) What is the name for the Mediterranean wind that originates from the Sahara, before travelling across North Africa and into Southern Europe?

8) There are two 'Newcastles' in England; Newcastle upon Tyne and Newcastle...?

9) The former country of Upper Volta is now known as what?

10) The Magellan Strait is at the bottom of which continent?

Quiz 39 – Answers

1) Frank Carson, 2) David Coleman, 3) Sarah Burton (working for the fashion label Alexander McQueen), 4) Post Impressionism, 5) The three unforgivable curses, 6) Captain America, 7) 50mph, 8) Luke Skywalker, 9) Benny Goodman, 10) Alan Parry

Quiz 42 - General Knowledge

1) What is the currency of Brazil?

2) What was the famous English landscape architect Capability Brown's first name?

3) How many letters are there in the Greek alphabet?

4) Which English football team is known as the Tangerines?

5) What does the adage Murphy's Law state?

6) What type of animal is a Flying Fox?

7) Which art movement is Pablo Picasso most associated with, which was popular around the 1900's to 1910's?

8) What is the largest island in the world?

9) Which country usually leads the parade of participants in the opening and closing ceremonies at the Olympic Games?

10) Who was the original voice of the animation 'Bob the Builder'?

Quiz 40 – Answers

1) Choux, 2) Escudo, 3) Aladdin, 4) Davy Crocket, 5) Queens Park Rangers, 6) Viscount, 7) Europe, 8) Nevada, 9) Juliet, 10) Guernica

Quiz 43 - History and Politics

1) After abdication, Edward VIII became governor of where?

2) "Four score and seven years ago" was the start of which famous speech?

3) What is the name of the mythical ship that supposedly can never make port and so will sail the seas forever, The Flying...?

4) Richard III was the last English King to die in battle, but at which battle was he killed? (He was not the last British king to be killed in battle though).

5) Famous for pioneering aviation and powered flight, what were the Wright brothers' first names?

6) The charge of the light brigade was part of which battle?

7) What was the nickname of Manfred Freiherr von Richthofen, the most famous German fighter pilot of World War I?

8) 'Copenhagen' was the name of whose horse?

9) In which decade did the Republic of Ireland gain independence?

10) What earthwork marked the boundary between the Kingdom of Mercia and Wales?

Quiz 41 – Answers

1) Matlock, 2) Solomon Islands, 3) Ivory Coast, 4) Rotterdam, 5) St Lawrence River, 6) Kamchatka Peninsula, 7) Sirocco, 8)Under-Lyme, 9) Burkina Faso, 10) South America

1) What is the name of the world heritage site castle on the island of Anglesey?

2) What was Margaret Thatcher's maiden name?

3) 'MSN' was an abbreviation used for which three of F.C Barcelona's attacking trio from 2014 to 2017?

4) What is the name for a rich shellfish soup often made using lobster?

5) Who was the second person to walk on the moon?

6) What is the chemical symbol for Iron in the periodic table?

7) What is P. Diddy's real name?

8) Who was the Roman goddess of flowers and spring?

9) Pireaus is the major port of which city?

10) At what address did Sherlock Holmes live?

Quiz 42 – Answers

1) The Brazilian real, 2) Lancelot, 3) 24, 4) Blackpool, 5) Anything that can go wrong will go wrong, 6) A bat, 7) Cubism, 8) Greenland (Australia is considered a continent), 9) Greece. 10) Neil Morrissey

1) What is the term used for a seldom seen four under par in golf?

2) Which team in cricket is known as the Black Caps?

3) Who was the permanent (not Caretaker) manager of Arsenal F.C after George Graham but before Arsène Wenger?

4) The Americas cup is a trophy awarded in which sport?

5) Which race makes up the US Triple Crown along with the Kentucky Derby and Belmont stakes?

6) Earl Strickland is considered one of the greatest players of all time in which sport?

7) In which park in London were the Equestrian events held for the 2012 Olympics?

8) Which two football teams play at England's two closest football grounds?

9) In which city is the Italian Grand Prix held?

10) Which rugby team plays at the Twickenham Stoop Stadium?

Quiz 43 – Answers

1) The Bahamas, 2) Gettysburg Address, 3) Dutchman, 4) Battle of Bosworth Field, 5) Orville and Wilbur, 6) The Battle of Balaclava, 7) The Red Baron, 8) The Duke of Wellington, 9) 1920's, 10) Offa's Dyke

1) Vodka, triple sec, lime juice and cranberry juice are the ingredients of what famous cocktail?

2) What calendar did Britain use before the Gregorian calendar was adopted?

3) Who is Great Britain's most successful female Olympian?

4) How many secondary colours are there and can you name them?

5) The Tyrannosaurus Rex is believed to have lived in which modern day continent?

6) Which famous novel series did Stephanie Meyer write?

7) Before being overthrown by the United States, Queen Liliuokalani was the last monarch of where?

8) Which European country is divided up into 'cantons'?

9) The Jules Rimet Trophy was awarded in which sport?

10) What is the name of the animated series of comedy short films produced by Warner Bros which included characters such as Bugs Bunny, Daffy Duck, and Tweety?

Quiz 44 – Answers

1) Beaumaris Castle, 2) Roberts, 3) Messi, Suarez, Neymar, 4) Bisque, 5) Buzz Aldrin, 6) Fe, 7) Sean Combs, 8) Flora, 9) Athens, 10) 221b Baker Street

Quiz 47 - Science and Nature

1) What is Thomas A. Swift's Electric Rifle better known as?

2) Which two planets in our solar system do not have moons?

3) What is the only living relative of the giraffe species, which was also one of the last discovered large mammals?

4) The two main ways of measuring the strength and intensity of earthquakes are using the Richter scale and which other scale?

5) Rickets can be caused by the deficiency of what vitamin?

6) How many pairs of ribs does an adult human have?

7) What is the term for a ring shaped reef comprised largely of coral?

8) What is the third most abundant gas in the earth's atmosphere after Nitrogen and Oxygen?

9) What is the name for a tree that sheds its leaves at the end of the season, usually autumn?

10) Oology is the study of what?

Quiz 45 – Answers

1) Condor, 2) New Zealand, 3) Bruce Rioch, 4) Sailing, 5) Preakness Stakes, 6) Pool (9 ball), 7) Greenwich park, 8) Nottingham Forest and Notts County, 9) Monza, 10) Harlequins

1) What is the only U.S state to begin with 'A' but not end in 'A'?

2) What was the name of the Queen's cousin who the IRA assassinated with a bomb while he was fishing in Ireland in 1979?

3) Which city in 2022 will become the first city to ever host both the Winter and Summer Olympics?

4) Which drinking spirit comes from the Blue Agave plant?

5) What is zero degrees Celsius in Fahrenheit?

6) Keith Moon was a famous drummer with which band?

7) What was Malcolm Little more famously known as?

8) Zealand is the largest island of which country?

9) Ice Hockey and which other sport are said to be the national sports of Canada?

10) Which author penned Paradise Lost?

Quiz 46 – Answers

1) Cosmopolitan, 2) Julian Calendar, 3) Laura Trott (subsequently named Laura Kenny after marriage), 4) Three- Purple, Green, Orange, 5) North America, 6) Twilight, 7) Hawaii, 8) Switzerland, 9) Football, 10) Looney Tunes

Quiz 49 - The Arts and Entertainment

1) This BBC sitcom show ran from 2001 to 2011 and starred Ralph Little. Complete the title; "Two pints of lager and a…"?

2) Who wrote the famous novel 'A Brave New World'?

3) What is the occupation of the man who turns into the incredible hulk?

4) What is the name of the alphabet used in Russia and by other Slavic people?

5) What is the name of Captain Pugwash's ship?

6) Who wrote Robinson Crusoe?

7) In the film `The Matrix`, by what name is Keanu Reeve`s character Thomas A. Anderson known?

8) Who was elected in 2009 to become the first ever female British Poet Laureate?

9) Who wrote `The Strange Case of Dr Jeckyll and Mr Hyde`?

10) In which fictional Melbourne suburb is the soap opera 'Neighbours' set?

Quiz 47 – Answers

1) A Taser, 2) Mercury and Venus, 3) The Okapi, 4) Mercalli scale, 5) Vitamin D, 6) Twelve, 7) An 'Atoll', 8) Argon, 9) Deciduous, 10) Birds eggs

Quiz 50 - General Knowledge

1) Switzerland's official languages are French, Italian, German and which other?

2) What happened on the 15 February 1971 in the UK?

3) Which alcohol is primarily used in a Singapore Sling?

4) Before a bout, what do sumo wrestlers throw into the ring?

5) A Bactrian Camel has one hump, and a dromedary camel has two humps. True or false?

6) What is the name of the major stock market index for the Tokyo Stock Exchange?

7) Who is the host of the TV show QI, replacing Stephen Fry?

8) Who overthrew Fulgenico Batista as part of a revolution in the 1950s?

9) Palermo is the capital of which island?

10) Valentine and Proteus feature in which Shakespeare play?

Quiz 48 – Answers

1) Arkansas, 2) Lord Louis Mountbatton, 3) Beijing, 4) Tequila, 5) 32, 6) The Who, 7) Malcolm X, 8) Denmark, 9) Lacrosse, 10) John Milton

1) Port au Prince is the capital of which French speaking Caribbean Island?

2) Which is the largest of Canada's islands?

3) What famous landmark is situated within the Black Hills range in the US?

4) The Taurus Mountains are in which country?

5) What is the name of the Russian enclave situated between Poland and Lithuania?

6) There are three countries in the world completely surrounded by one other country. Name them.

7) What is the largest country in Africa by area?

8) Situated in the North Island, which is the largest lake in New Zealand?

9) Which London tube line goes through Paddington, Oxford Circus, and Elephant and Castle?

10) Firenze is the name of which city in the local language?

Quiz 49 – Answers

1) Packet of Crisps, 2) Aldous Huxley, 3) Scientist, 4) Cyrillic, 5) The Black Pig, 6) Daniel Defoe, 7) Neo, 8) Carol Ann Duffy, 9) Robert Louis Stevenson, 10) Erinsborough

1) Which country has the largest natural gas reserves in the world?

2) Which US president invented the Lightning Conductor?

3) Who was the manager of Manchester United before Sir Alex Ferguson?

4) What is the study of cancer known as?

5) How do you write 1985 in Roman numerals?

6) Mark Knopfler is the lead singer of which band?

7) A sliotar is a ball used in which sport?

8) What was Operation Dynamo?

9) In which U.S state is Death Valley?

10) What is the book of quotations from Chairman Mao Tse-tung commonly known as?

Quiz 50 – Answers

1) Romansch, 2) Decimalisation, 3) Gin, 4) Salt, 5) False, the other way round, 6) Nikkei, 7) Sandi Toksvig, 8) Fidel Castro, 9) Sicily, 10) The Two Gentlemen Of Verona

1) What was the name of the main German defensive line in World War I?

2) Which revolutionary is known as the founding father of the Republic of China?

3) What is the oldest continuously inhabited city in the world?

4) Who was the Greek messenger of the gods?

5) The 'Louisiana purchase' which was made by the USA, was from which other country?

6) What was the name of the prison in Germany which for a period had only one prisoner- the Nazi war Criminal Rudoloph Hess?

7) Which English king was killed by an arrow in a hunting accident?

8) The Titanic had two sister ships, can you name either of them?

9) Which famous British general was killed during the Siege of Khartoum?

10) What was the name of the largest ship used by Christopher Columbus on his first voyage to the Caribbean?

Quiz 51 – Answers

1) Haiti, 2) Baffin island, 3) Mount Rushmore, 4) Turkey, 5) Kalingrad, 6) Lesotho, San Marino, Vatican City, 7) Algeria, 8) Lake Taupo, 9)Bakerloo line, 10) Florence

1) The Galapagos Islands belong to which country?

2) Which hot drink derives its name from the colour of the hooded robes worn by monks and nuns of the Capuchin order?

3) What was the name of the Egyptian President who was assassinated in 1981?

4) What is the Cresta Run?

5) What was the name of the project that created the world's first nuclear weapons?

6) Which fast food chain has the most restaurants in the world?

7) What was the name of Bob Marley's backing band?

8) Omega Pharma-Quick Step was a team name competing in which sport?

9) Which amendment to the US constitution allows the 'right to bear arms'?

10) From what 1985 film is the line "Roads? Where we're going we don't need roads."

Quiz 52 – Answers

1) Russia, 2) Benjamin Franklin, 3) Ron Atkinson, 4) Oncology, 5) MCMLXXXV, 6) Dire Straits, 7) Hurling, 8) The evacuation of the British forces at Dunkirk during World War II, 9) California, 10) The little Red Book

Quiz 55 - Sport and Leisure

1) In cricket, how many overs must be completed in a test match before the first new ball is due?

2) In the 1966 world cup final win for England, Geoff Hurst famously scored a 'hat trick' in the 4-2 win, but who scored the other goal for England?

3) How high should the centre of a dartboard be from the ground?

4) Which is the highest altitude football ground in the English League?

5) A full house beats four of a kind in poker, true or false?

6) What are the first names of British ice dancers Torvill and Dean?

7) What does NASCAR stand for in the American car racing events?

8) In what decade was the first Rugby Union World Cup?

9) What nationality is golfer Vijay Singh?

10) Which German football team plays at the Westfalenstadion stadium?

Quiz 53 – Answers

1) Hindenburg Line, 2) Sun Yat Sen, 3) Damascus, Syria, 4) Hermes, 5) France, 6) Spandeu, 7) William II, 8) Britannic, Olympic, 9) General Gordan, 10) Santa Maria

1) What is a Norfolk Bronze?

2) In which country is El Alamein, famous for two World War II battles?

3) In which city is the 'Hibs' football team based?

4) What type of animal is a Portuguese man o' war?

5) Who played Jim Royle in the sitcom 'The Royle Family'?

6) Which city has hosted the summer Olympics the most times?

7) Which metal do you get from bauxite?

8) Who did Mark Chapman famously shoot in 1980 in New York?

9) Sacramento is the capital of which U.S state?

10) Who is the lead singer of the Boomtown Rats?

Quiz 54 – Answers

1) Ecuador, 2) Cappuccino, 3) Anwar Saddat, 4) A famous toboggan track at St Moritz, 5) Manhattan Project, 6) Subway, 7) The Wailers, 8) Road cycling, 9) Second amendment, 10)'Back to the Future'

Quiz 57 - Science and Nature

1) Where is the Cassini division?

2) Who invented the Periodic table?

3) What is Frank Wittle famous for inventing?

4) Who first discovered that the earth revolves around the sun?

5) Which animal's name comes from the ancient Greek for "river horse"?

6) How many feet are in a fathom?

7) What is the name of the pigment that is the primary determinant of skin colour?

8) What is the term for a breast x-ray?

9) Name either of Mars' two moons?

10) Which engineer designed the first VW beetle?

Quiz 55 – Answers

1) 80, 2) Martin Peters, 3) 5 foot 8 inches, 4) The Hawthorns (West Bromwich Albion), 5) False, 6) Jayne and Christopher, 7) National Association for Stock Car Auto Racing, 8) 1980's (1987), 9) Fijian, 10) Dortmund

1) Where Eggs Benedict uses ham, what does Eggs Royale use?

2) The Grand Canyon is in which U.S state?

3) Which two brothers invented the hot air balloon?

4) What is significant about the Olympic events of synchronized swimming and rhythmic gymnastics?

5) When are the twelve days of Christmas?

6) Who was the original host of the TV show 'The Crystal Maze'?

7) The constellation Ursa Major is also known as what?

8) Who was the lead singer of Black Sabbath?

9) The Punic wars were fought between which two military powers?

10) Under what name was Superman raised as a child?

Quiz 56 – Answers

1) A breed of Turkey, 2) Egypt, 3) Edinburgh, 4) Jellyfish, 5) Ricky Tomlinson, 6) London (three times; 1908, 1948 and 2012), 7) Aluminium, 8) John Lennon, 9) California, 10) Bob Geldof

Quiz 59 - The Arts and Entertainment

1) What are the names of the three Musketeers in the historical novel by Alexandre Dumas?

2) What was the name of the official newspaper of the Communist Party of the Soviet Union?

3) Name either of the James bond films starring Timothy Dalton?

4) The architect Renzo Piano designed which iconic London building which was completed in 2012?

5) Which famous singer-songwriter was married to Maurice Gibb of the Bee Gees from 1969-1973?

6) Who painted the famous 'portrait of Henry VIII'?

7) Which comic book hero has a mighty hammer called Mjolnir?

8) What species is Chewbacca in the Star Wars films?

9) What is the name of the sequel film to 'Bourne Identity'?

10) In which country was Gloria Estefan born?

Quiz 57 – Answers

1) In the rings of Saturn, 2) Dmitri Mendeleev, 3) The jet engine, 4) Copernicus, 5) Hippopotamus, 6) 7) Melanin, 8) Mammogram, 9) Phobos and Deimos, 10) Ferdinand Porsche (the founder of Porsche Car Company)

Quiz 60 - General Knowledge

1) How did the famous American and French dancer of the early 20th Century, Isadora Duncan, die?

2) The River Po is the longest river in which country?

3) Throughout the whole of the 14th century, the tallest building in the world was in the UK, what was it?

4) In tenpin bowling, what is a Turkey?

5) Which metal has the highest conductivity of all metals?

6) Which country is the potato dish 'Rösti from?

7) Who played 'Baldrick' in the Blackadder sitcom?

8) Who did Gavrilo Princip assassinate, which lead to the outbreak of World War I?

9) Which sport is played on the largest pitch?

10) In the Bible, who was the third son of Adam and Eve, after Cain and Abel?

Quiz 58 – Answers

1) Smoked Salmon, 2) Arizona, 3) Montgolfier brothers, 4) They are the only two events which are only competed for by women, 5) December 25th to January 6th, 6) Richard O'Brien, 7) The Great Bear, 8) Ozzy Osbourne, 9) Rome and Carthage, 10) Clark Kent

1) Which waterfall is made up of three separate waterfalls, the largest of which is named Horseshoe Falls?

2) Melbourne is the capital of which Australian state?

3) What is the name of the River Thames when it runs through Oxford?

4) What is the tallest mountain on mainland contiguous USA?

5) What is the largest entirely Indonesian island?

6) What is the name of the strait between Anglesey and mainland Wales?

7) Where is Ronaldsway Airport situated?

8) What is the official name of the tower where Big Ben is situated?

9) What is the collective term for the historic series of coastal towns in Kent and Sussex, made up of Hastings, New Romney, Hythe, Dover and Sandwich?

10) What is the deepest point in the Earth's oceans?

Quiz 59 – Answers

1) Aramis, Athos and Porthos, 2) Pravda, 3) The Living Daylights or License to Kill, 4) The Shard, 5) Lulu, 6) Hans Holbein the Younger, 7) Thor, 8) Wookie, 9) Bourne Supremacy, 10) Cuba

Quiz 62 - General Knowledge

1) Where do the Flintstones live?

2) 'Lusitania' refers to which European country?

3) What was the name of the river which Julius Caesar crossed with his troops to initiate a civil war?

4) How many points do you need to win a squash game?

5) What is the longest river in the British Isles? Hint: this is not the same as the longest river in the UK.

6) What was the first country to give women the vote?

7) Which was the last host nation to win the FIFA World Cup (as of 2020)?

8) What animal does vulpine refer to?

9) What was the name of the spin-off series to Doctor Who, which aired for four series between 2006 to 2011?

10) In the film 'The Silence of the Lambs', which actor played the part of Hannibal Lector?

Quiz 60 – Answers

1) Her scarf became entangled in the wheel of the car she was riding in, 2) Italy, 3) Lincoln cathedral, 4) Three strikes in a row, 5) Silver, 6) Switzerland, 7) Tony Robinson, 8) Archduke Franz Ferdinand, 9) Polo, 10) Seth

Quiz 63 - History and Politics

1) The Kinder Scout mass trespass was in which national park?

2) The world's first female Prime Minister was in which country?

3) Name the two animals that complete the names of the leaders of two Sioux tribes: Crazy... and Sitting...?

4) Which German General was nicknamed 'The desert fox'?

5) What was the name of the civilian massacre by American soldiers in Vietnam in 1968?

6) What was the name of Napolean's horse?

7) Who founded the Republic of Turkey?

8) 'Pickles' was the name of the dog that found what stolen item under a bush in London in 1966?

9) What was the name of the organisation set up after the First World War which was the predecessor to United Nations?

10) Who was said to be the 'Wisest Fool in Christendom'?

Quiz 61 – Answers

1) Niagara Falls, 2) Victoria, 3) The Isis, 4) Mount Whitney, 5) Sumatra, 6) Menai Strait, 7) Isle of Man, 8) The Elizabeth Tower, 9) Cinque Ports, 10) Mariana Trench

1) ABBA won the Eurovision Song Contest in 1974 with which song?

2) Which country is Red Stripe lager from?

3) Famous for subsequently creating the Boy Scouts organisation, who was the British commander at the Siege of Mafeking during the Second Boer War?

4) Which country is the largest producer of coffee in the world?

5) What is Batman's real name?

6) Expeditions on Mount Ararat have searched for what biblical object, due to the mountain supposedly being its final resting place?

7) Which famous derby winning racehorse was kidnapped in 1983, never to be seen again?

8) What fruit is a prune made from?

9) What is a female donkey called?

10) Who directed the film The Pianist, and was also the former husband of Sharon Tate?

Quiz 62 – Answers

1) Bedrock, 2) Portugal, 3) The Rubicon, 4) Eleven, 5) River Shannon, 6) New Zealand, 7) France (1998), 8) Fox, 9) Torchwood, 10) Anthony Hopkins

1) Which club was Manchester United on the way back from playing, when the Munich air disaster happened in 1958? Hint: It wasn't Bayern Munich!

2) With a trophy now named after him, William Webb Ellis is credited as the inventor of which sport?

3) Which golfer is known as the `Great White Shark`?

4) Which English Premier League football club is said to be one of the only grounds in the world (if not the only ground) to have a church (St. Luke the Evangelist) in the corner of the stadium?

5) Who was the first ever person to hit two nine dart finishes in the same darts match in 2010?

6) What is former English Cricketer David Lloyd's nickname?

7) What was the first US city to host the Olympics in 1904?

8) Who holds the record for the longest hitting streak in Major League Baseball history?

9) Where does The St Leger Stakes take place every year?

10) There are three types of sword used in fencing? Epee, sabre and which other...?

Quiz 63 – Answers

1) The Peak District, 2) Sri Lanka, 3) Crazy Horse and Sitting Bull, 4) Erwin Rommel, 5) My Lai, 6) Marengo, 7) Mustafa Kemal Atatürk, 8) Jules Rimet football World Cup trophy, 9) The League of Nations, 10) James I of England

1) Fill in the missing US president: Carter, [.....], Bush, Clinton.

2) Which sport is said to be the 'Sport of Kings'?

3) Name any of the five London Underground Tube stations that are named after pubs?

4) Robert Zimmerman is the birth name of which famous singer?

5) What is the international telephone calling code for France?

6) What is the third longest river in the world after the Nile and the Amazon?

7) Who is the only ever British Prime Minister to be assassinated?

8) The Chicago Cubs play what sport?

9) Saskatchewan is a province in which country?

10) On the sixth day of Christmas what did my true love give to me?

Quiz 64 – Answers

1) Waterloo, 2) Jamaica, 3) Robert Baden Powell, 4) Brazil, 5) Bruce Wayne, 6) Noah's ark, 7) Shergar, 8) Plum, 9) A Jenny, 10) Roman Polanski

1) What term is used for a unit of time that is shorter than an eon but longer than a period?

2) Name any of the three parts of the small intestine?

3) Which element has the chemical symbol Mn?

4) Charles Babbage is famous for being the 'father' of what, having created one of the first versions of this item?

5) Who designed the biological classification system that is currently used?

6) What is the base measurement for describing luminous intensity? Hint: it's not Lumens or Lux.

7) Which protein forms hair and nails?

8) In computing, the initials 'GUI' stand for what?

9) For an equine to be considered a horse rather than a pony, how many hands must it be?

10) What do you measure with a barometer?

Quiz 65 – Answers

1) Red Star Belgrade, 2) Rugby, 3) Greg Norman, 4) Everton, 5) Phil Taylor, 6) 'Bumble', 7) St. Louis, 8) Joe DiMaggio, 9) Doncaster, 10 Foil

1) What is the name given to the succession of streets linking Edinburgh Castle and Holyrood Palace?

2) Haile Selassie was the Regent of which country before he was deposed?

3) What is John Pemberton famous for creating?

4) Which English runner held the female world record marathon time for 16 years, until it was broken in 2019?

5) Lemonade and what other ingredient makes a snowball cocktail?

6) What is the phonetic alphabet word for 'U'?

7) What is the only venomous snake in Britain?

8) Who painted the Hay Wain?

9) Which major river runs through New York City?

10) Pete Best was a member of which band, but left before they became famous?

Quiz 66 – Answers

1) Reagan, 2) Horse Racing, 3) Royal Oak, Elephant and Castle, Angel, Manor House, Swiss Cottage, 4) Bob Dylan, 5) +33, 6) Yangtze River, 7) Spencer Perceval, 8) Baseball, 9) Canada, 10) 6 geese a-laying

Quiz 69 - The Arts and Entertainment

1) Which popular marvel comic hero was blinded in a freak accident?

2) The character Max Rockatansky features in which films?

3) Who wrote the novel 'Frankenstein'?

4) How is Major Boothroyd better known?

5) In English, what is the Welsh national anthem called?

6) Pharrell Williams was part of which band before he became a solo artist?

7) "You talkin' to me" is a line said by Robert De Niro in which film?

8) In which city is the oldest university in Europe?

9) The Battle of Agincourt features in which Shakespeare play?

10) With which band is Fred Durst the lead singer?

Quiz 67 – Answers

1) Era, 2) Duodenum, jejunum, ileum, 3) Manganese, 4) Computers, 5) Carl Linneaeus, 6) Candela, 7) Keratin, 8) Graphical User Interface, 9) 14.2 or more, 10) Atmospheric pressure

Quiz 70 - General Knowledge

1) What colour is the black box in an aircraft?

2) Colonel Thomas Blood is best known for his attempt to steal what?

3) Doge's Palace is a major landmark in which city?

4) Norma Jeane Mortenson was the given name of which famous actor?

5) Prior to 1996, the Indian city of Chennai was known as what?

6) Which two teams were playing football when the Hillsborough disaster happened?

7) In which city are the headquarters of Interpol?

8) How is Richard Starkey better known?

9) Who invented dynamite?

10) A qualified airline pilot, Bruce Dickinson is the lead singer of which band?

Quiz 68 – Answers

1) The Royal Mile, 2) Ethiopia, 3) Coca Cola, 4) Paula Radcliffe, 5) Advocaat, 6) Uniform, 7) The Adder, 8) John Constable, 9) The Hudson River, 10) The Beatles

1) Situated in Asia, which capital city is the coldest in the world?

2) Which river has the capitals of both Uruguay and Argentina on its banks?

3) Which is the second largest city in Austria after Vienna? Hint: it's not Salzburg or Innsbruck.

4) The island of Socotra in the Arabian Sea belongs to which country?

5) What is the tallest mountain in Canada?

6) Which river runs through Baghdad?

7) Which airport was originally known as Ringway airport?

8) Residents of which Caribbean island had to be evacuated after a dormant volcano became active in 1995?

9) Edo, is the former name of which Asian city?

10) What is the largest city in Alaska?

Quiz 69 – Answers

1) Daredevil, 2) Mad Max, 3) Mary Shelley, 4) Q in the James bond stories, 5) Old Land of My Fathers, 6) N.E.R.D, 7) Taxi Driver, 8) Bologna, 9) Henry V, 10) Limp Bizkit

Quiz 72 - General Knowledge

1) What are 'Angels on Horseback'?

2) Antarctica is said to be the largest desert in the world, but what is the world's largest hot desert?

3) Ceylon is the former name for which country?

4) Whose long-jump record in the 1968 Olympics lasted for almost 23 years?

5) Who directed the film Titanic?

6) By what name was Sir Arthur Wellesley also known?

7) Who painted the famous painting known as 'The Persistence of Memory'?

8) Which cricket team plays its home matches at Lords?

9) Which is the largest type of penguin?

10) By what name is the superhero Peter Parker also known?

Quiz 70 – Answers

1) Orange, 2) The Crown jewels, 3) Venice, 4) Marilyn Monroe, 5) Madras, 6) Liverpool and Nottingham Forest, 7) Lyon, 8) Ringo Starr, 9) Alfred Nobel, 10) Iron Maiden

1) What was the name of the Nazi war criminal who was kidnapped in 1960 by Israeli secret agents in Argentina to be trialled in Israel?

2) The Treaty of Waitangi was signed in which country?

3) With which ship did Francis Drake become the first Englishman to circumnavigate the globe?

4) Along with Cavour and Mazzini, who is famous for being one of the founding fathers of Italy?

5) Which Treaty ended the American Revolution?

6) Who was the leader of Japan during World War II?

7) In 1743 George II led his troops into which battle, becoming the last British monarch to do so?

8) Who invented the helicopter?

9) Jonestown, a settlement famous for a mass suicide and massacre in the 1970's, is in which country?

10) Custer's last stand occurred in which battle?

Quiz 71 – Answers

1) Ulaanbaatar, 2) The River Plate, 3) Graz, 4) Yemen, 5) Mount Logan, 6) Tigris river, 7) Manchester Airport, 8) Monserrat, 9) Tokyo, 10) Anchorage

Quiz 74 - General Knowledge

1) On which city's train network could you go from South Gosforth to West Jesmond?

2) Which of the following events happened first; Princess Diana killed in a car crash, Channel 5 launched, or the Channel Tunnel opened?

3) What did the media nickname the ex RBS CEO Fred Goodwin?

4) In which river did Achilles' mother reputedly dip him by the heel?

5) How many points is the brown ball worth in Snooker?

6) What is the fifth letter of the Greek alphabet?

7) What do you get if you order pomme de terre in France?

8) Which country's cars have the international vehicle registration code of the letter 'CH'?

9) Also the voice of Wallace in Wallace and Gromit films, Peter Sallis starred in which long running sitcom?

10) What is also known as 'La Giocondo' in Italian?

Quiz 72 – Answers

1) A dish of Oysters wrapped in bacon, 2) The Sahara desert, 3) Sri Lanka, 4) Bob Beamon's, 5) James Cameron, 6) The Duke of Wellington, 7) Salvador Dali, 8) Middlesex, 9) Emperor Penguin, 10) Spiderman

1) In badminton, how many points do you need to win a game?

2) Fill in the missing Champion's League winning team: Internazionale, Barcelona, [.....], Bayern Munich, Real Madrid.

3) Heather Mckay is an Australian sportswoman, arguably the greatest ever, who completely dominated which sport during the 1960's and 1970's? She went unbeaten from 1962 to 1981 and won 16 consecutive British Open titles.

4) Which jockey won the 1970 St Leger Stakes on Nijinsky?

5) What sport do the Philadelphia Eagles play?

6) Which English county has Brian Lara played cricket for?

7) Where is Ballaugh Bridge, which features in a famous race each year?

8) In 1976 in Montreal, Romanian athlete Nadia Comaneci became the first person in Olympic history to do what?

9) Cardiff Football Club used which stadium as their home ground for 99 years before moving to the Cardiff City Stadium?

10) The 1956 Olympics were hosted by Melbourne, but due to quarantine regulations, the equestrian events were held where?

Quiz 73 – Answers

1) Adolf Eichmann, 2) New Zealand, 3) The Golden Hind, 4) Giuseppe Garibaldi, 5) Treaty of Paris, 6) Emperor Hirohito, 7) Battle of Dettingen, 8) Igor Sikorsky, 9) Guyana, 10) Battle of Little Bighorn

Quiz 76 - General Knowledge

1) What is the highest altitude capital city in Europe?

2) What is the name of the ship used by the pilgrims in 1620 to travel to 'the new world'?

3) Which was the first British football team to win the European Cup?

4) King Zog was the monarch of which European country from 1922-1939?

5) Which two actors starred in the TV comedy series 'Men Behaving Badly'?

6) What is the symbol of Sagittarius?

7) What does the 'P' and 'O' stand for in the cruise line 'P&O Cruises'?

8) Which former Liberal Democrat politician had a relationship with pop star Gabriela Irimia of 'The Cheeky girls'?

9) Who fought Muhammed Ali in the "Rumble in The Jungle"?

10) Which British peerage is between Earl and Duke?

Quiz 74 – Answers

1) Newcastle, 2) Channel Tunnel opened,1994, Channel 5 launched, March 1997, Princess Diana killed, August 1997, 3) 'Fred the Shred', 4) River Styx, 5) 4, 6) Epsilon, 7) Potato, 8) Switzerland, 9) Last of The Summer Wine, 10) The Mona Lisa painting

1) What is the SI unit of frequency?

2) What geological epoch are we currently living in?

3) What is a female deer called?

4) How is the disease Varicella better known?

5) Called Olympus Mons, on which planet is the tallest mountain in the Solar System?

6) If you mix 50ml of water with 50ml of ethanol, what volume of liquid will you have? 100ml, less than 100ml, or more than 100ml?

7) 'Dyspepsia' is more commonly known as what?

8) What is the collective name for a group of frogs?

9) Which element has the chemical symbol Co?

10) How many inches make up a hand?

Quiz 75 – Answers

1) 21, 2) Chelsea (2012), 3) Squash, 4) Lester Piggott, 5) American Football, 6) Warwickshire, 7) Isle of Man –it is part of the Isle of Man TT race, 8) Be awarded the first perfect score of ten in Gymnastics, 9) Ninian Park, 10) Stockholm, Sweden

Quiz 78 - General Knowledge

1) In which UK city is Albert Dock?

2) ETA, a separatist organization/terrorist group that disbanded recently, had promoted independence for which region in Europe?

3) What is the oldest current museum in the UK?

4) Where was the 2019 Rugby World Cup held? This was the first time the tournament has been held outside one of the 'major' rugby playing nations.

5) Who invented the television?

6) What is the name for a group of owls?

7) Who wrote the novel Les Miserables?

8) Denali, situated in Alaska, is the highest mountain peak in North America, but what was its former name before it was renamed in 2015?

9) What are teenagers Eric Harris and Dylan Klebold infamous for?

10) What comic book character does Bruce Banner turn into?

Quiz 76 – Answers

1) Madrid, 2) The Mayflower, 3) Celtic, 4) Albania, 5) Martin Clunes and Neil Morrissey, 6) The Archer, 7) Peninsular and Oriental, 8) Lembit Öpik,9) George Foreman, 10) Marquess

Quiz 79 - The Arts and Entertainment

1) What was the name of Peter Pan's closest friend?

2) What are the names of Harry Potter's parents?

3) What is the registration number on Lady Penelope's car in Thunderbirds?

4) Curtis Jackson is the real name of which rapper?

5) Who was the original host of the show Man v. Food?

6) William Hartnell was the first actor to play which famous TV character?

7) What is the name of the prominent art museum in Florence?

8) Who is the leader of the toys in Toy Story?

9) Who did James May replace on the BBC show 'Top Gear' for the second series onwards?

10) In the story, who carved Pinocchio?

Quiz 77 – Answers

1) Hertz (Hz), 2) The Holocene Epoch, 3) A doe, 4) Chickenpox, 5) Mars, 6) Less than 100ml (because the ethanol molecules are smaller than the water molecules so ethanol molecules fit themselves between the water molecules, making the liquid more dense yet the same mass, hence smaller volume), 7) Indigestion, 8) An army, 9) Cobalt, 10) 4

1) In which country is the Bay of Pigs?

2) What was the name of the tanker that suffered a severe oil spillage off the coast of Alaska in 1989?

3) What one word is usually said in Bingo, before announcing the number eleven?

4) What is the name of the diamond that forms part of the British Crown jewels, the ownership of which is disputed by India?

5) Canine refers to dogs, and ovine refers to what animal?

6) What is the most common name for a pub in the UK?

7) What is the name of the fictional east London Borough in Eastenders?

8) The metal of Russian cannons captured at the battle of Sevastopol was for a period used by the British to make what?

9) Which country has the largest proven oil reserves in the world as of 2018? Hint: it's not Saudi Arabia, who is the largest producer of oil.

10) What is the name of the warthog in the Lion King?

Quiz 78 – Answers

1) Liverpool, 2) Basque region, 3) The Ashmolean Museum, 4) Japan, 5) John Logie Baird, 6) A Parliament, 7) Victor Hugo, 8) Mount McKinley, 9) The 1999 Columbine High School Massacre, 10) The Incredible Hulk

1) California is nicknamed the Golden State, but which U.S state is nicknamed the Silver State?

2) Which country has the only non-rectangular flag currently in use?

3) Halifax is the capital of which Canadian province?

4) What is the name of the mountain range that runs through Morocco, Algeria, and Tunisia?

5) What is the alternative name for the island of Rapa Nui?

6) What is the most northerly capital city in the world?

7) Which explorer was the island of Tasmania named after?

8) The river Tiber runs through which major European capital?

9) Situated in Northern Ireland, which is the largest lake in the British Isles by surface area?

10) The second highest waterfall in the world, the Tugela Falls, is situated in which African country?

Quiz 79 – Answers

1) Tinker Bell, 2) James and Lily, 3) FAB 1, 4) 50 Cent, 5) Adam Richman, 6) Dr Who, 7) The Uffizi Gallery, 8) Woody, 9) Jason Dawe, 10) Geppetto

1) What was the 'Community Charge' more commonly known as?

2) What is the tallest mountain in South America, and also the highest mountain outside of Asia?

3) According to the Bible, how much did Judas receive for betraying Jesus?

4) How often does the Ryder cup take place?

5) Which two people became famous for their Nobel Prize winning studies on the structure of the human DNA?

6) What is the name of the blue chip stock market index consisting of the 30 major German companies trading on the Frankfurt Stock Exchange?

7) Who is the head of the Wimbledon burrow in the Wombles?

8) Helgoland is a small archipelago in the North Sea belonging to which country?

9) What was the name of the spin-off sitcom from Only Fools and Horses, starring Boycie?

10) In English, what is the UK Monarch's motto (outside of Scotland)?

Quiz 80 – Answers

1) Cuba, 2) Exxon Valdez, 3) Legs, 4) Koh-I-Noor, 5) Sheep, 6) The Red Lion, 7) Walford, 8) Victoria Cross medals, 9) Venezuela, 10) Pumbaa

1) Which country was previously known as New France?

2) What was the name of the British Royal Navy research vessel that James Cook sailed on for his first voyage to Australia and New Zealand?

3) A serious of prosecutions against people accused of witchcraft in Boston, USA came to be known as what?

4) In what year was the state of Israel formed?

5) What was the name of the Hull to Zeebrugge ferry which capsized in 1987, killing 193 people?

6) Black Bess was the name of which famous highwayman's horse?

7) What is 'Kristallnacht' also known as in English?

8) What was the name of the Venezuelan revolutionary leader who played a leading role in the establishment of many South American countries as sovereign states, independent of Spanish rule?

9) The 'Red Brigades', famous in the 1970's and 80's, operated in which country?

10) Who was the last Anglo-Saxon king of England, who fought William at the Battle of Hastings?

Quiz 81 – Answers

1) Nevada, 2) Nepal, 3) Nova Scotia, 4) The Atlas mountains, 5) Easter Island, 6) Reykjavik, 7) Abel Tasman, 8) Rome, 9) Lough Neagh, 10) South Africa

1) What is the tallest active volcano in Europe?

2) What is Cointreau a brand name of?

3) Who was the manager when England won the 1966 World Cup?

4) The Great fire of London destroyed around 80% of London, including 89 churches and 70,000 out of the 80,000 houses. But how many people did it kill? A) 6, B) 60, C) 600, or D) 6000.

5) What is the name of the café in Coronation Street?

6) A 'flutter' is the collective noun for which creature?

7) Who wrote the poem `The Owl and The Pussycat`?

8) Also famous for having a piece of clothing named after it, what was the name of the site where US atomic bomb testing took place?

9) With a famous street named after it, which is the largest of London's subterranean rivers?

10) Who created and produced the Star Wars films?

Quiz 82 – Answers

1) Poll Tax, 2) Aconcagua, 3) 30 pieces of silver, 4) Every two years, 5) Crick and Watson, 6) DAX, 7) Great Uncle Bulgaria, 8) Germany, 9) The Green Green Grass, 10) God and my right

1) The Stadium of Light is the name of two major football teams' grounds in Europe - Sunderland, and which other team?

2) What nationality is golfer Ernie Els?

3) The length of a cricket pitch is 22 yards, or 1 what?

4) Which commentator was known as 'The voice of darts' and now has the PDC world championship trophy named after him?

5) Losail International Circuit is a motor racing circuit in which country?

6) Where is Becher's Brook?

7) Which Arsenal footballer was nicknamed 'The Non-flying Dutchman' due to his fear of flying?

8) What is the name of the famous fell walker and author of multiple walking guides including a guide to the Pennine Way?

9) Which side has won the Super League title in Rugby league the most times?

10) Where is the Queen's Park Oval? The ground has hosted more cricket Test matches than any other ground in the Caribbean.

Quiz 83 – Answers

1) Canada, 2) HMS Endeavour, 3) The Salem Witch trials, 4) 1948, 5) Herald of Free Enterprise, 6) Dick Turpin, 7) The 'Night of the broken glass', 8) Simon Bolivar, 9) Italy, 10) Harold Godwinson

1) Which country's flag features an eagle and a snake?

2) Fletcher Christian and William Bligh were famous passengers on which ship?

3) The Claret Jug is a famous trophy in which sport?

4) A young male horse is a colt, but what do you call a young female horse?

5) What does the adage Parkinson's Law state?

6) Which actress married Prince Rainier of Monaco?

7) Who was the president and Head of State of Germany before Adolf Hitler?

8) In which city is Sugar Loaf Mountain?

9) What is the name of a period of play in a game of polo?

10) What is Norman Cook's stage name?

Quiz 84 – Answers

1) Mount Etna, 2) Triple sec, 3) Alf Ramsey, 4) A- 6, 5) Roy's Rolls, 6) Butterfly, 7) Edward Lear, 8) Bikini Atoll, 9) The River Fleet, 10) George Lucas

Quiz 87 - Science and Nature

1) What do you call a male swan?

2) Who accompanied Neil Armstrong and Buzz Aldrin on their trip to first walk on the moon?

3) What does the Beaufort scale measure?

4) What is the scientific name for the jawbone?

5) What is the name for a unit of length equivalent to 3.26 light years?

6) What do you call the home of a Badger?

7) Triton is which planet's largest moon?

8) Do objects appear smaller or larger when looking at them through a concave lens?

9) What is the name of the case on a ship where the navigational instruments are placed, such as the compass?

10) What is the name for a crack in a glacier?

Quiz 85 – Answers

1) Benfica, 2) South African, 3) 1 Chain, 4) Sid Waddell, 5) Qatar, 6) Aintree- it is a fence jumped over in the Grand National, 7) Dennis Bergkamp, 8) Alfred Wainwright, 9) Leeds Rhinos, 10) Port of Spain, Trinidad

89

1) How many stripes are there on the flag of the United States?

2) Where were the 10 commandments supposedly delivered to Moses by God?

3) In the British royal family, who did Prince Andrew marry in 1986?

4) Where did the 1976 Summer Olympics take place?

5) Which letter is in between G and J on a standard computer keyboard?

6) When put in order, which is the last sign of the Zodiac?

7) What is the brightest star in our night sky?

8) Hollyoaks is a fictional suburb of what city?

9) Which river runs through Amsterdam, and also gives its name to a famous Dutch beer?

10) Who is the alter ego of Paul O`Grady?

Quiz 86 – Answers

1) Mexico, 2) The Bounty, 3) Golf (the winner of The Open Championship receives it), 2) A filly, 3) Work expands so as to fill the time available for its completion, 4) Grace Kelly, 5) Paul Von Hindenburg, 6) Rio De Janeiro, 7) Chukka, 8) Fatboy Slim

1) Which William Golding novel focuses on a group of boys stranded on an uninhabited island, with characters named Jack, Piggy and Ralph?

2) On what Island was Freddie Mercury born?

3) What was the pen name of Eric Arthur Blair?

4) After leaving Oasis, what is the name of Liam Gallagher's new band?

5) Skaar, is the son of which famous superhero?

6) Which 1996 part-animated film featured basketball player Michael Jordan starring alongside Bugs Bunny?

7) What were Julius Caesar's last words (according to the Shakespeare play at least)?

8) What was the name of Kylie Minogue's character in Neighbours?

9) Nat king Cole is famous for playing which instrument?

10) What is Postman Pat`s surname?

Quiz 87 – Answers

1) A cob, 2) Michael Collins, 3) Wind speed, 4) Mandible, 5) A parsec, 6) A sett, 7) Neptune, 8) Smaller, 9) A binnacle,10) A crevasse

Quiz 90 - General Knowledge

1) Which London underground line would you use to go to Heathrow Airport?

2) What is J.D Salinger's most famous novel?

3) Who was supposedly the first person to circumnavigate the globe?

4) In traditional lore, there are eight reindeers pulling Santa Claus' sleigh; Dasher, Dancer, Prancer, Vixen, Comet, Cupid, Donner and which other?

5) What does the W stand for in George W Bush's name?

6) Sheffield FC is known as the oldest football club in the world, but which team is the oldest club in the Football League?

7) In the TV series `Only Fools And Horses`, what is the name of Boycie`s wife?

8) What is Pumpernickel a type of?

9) The Mosconi Cup takes place in which sport?

10) The famous line "Frankly, my dear, I don't give a damn" is from which film?

Quiz 88 – Answers

1) 13 - One for each independence declaring colony, 2) Mount Sinai, 3) Sarah Ferguson, 4) Montreal, 5) H, 6) Pisces, 7) Sirius A (Dog Star), 8) Chester, 9) Amstel, 10) Lily Savage

Quiz 91 - Geography

1) The largest city in the world located below sea level, and also the lowest capital city in the world, is in which central Asian country?

2) What is the longest river in North America? Hint: it's not the Mississippi River.

3) What is the capital of Tasmania?

4) The second tallest mountain in the world, 'K2', is situated on the border between which two countries?

5) Which country, as of 2020, is the largest producer of silver in the world?

6) The region of 'Puntland' is in which country?

7) In which country is the deepest lake in the world, which is also the world's largest freshwater lake?

8) Which country has the most active volcanoes in the world?

9) With a breed of dog sharing its name, what is the largest desert in North America?

10) Which American city is nicknamed 'Mile High City'?

Quiz 89 – Answers

1) Lord of the Flies, 2) Zanzibar, 3) George Orwell, 4) Beady Eye, 5) Hulk, 6) Space Jam, 7) `Et tu, Brute`, 8) Charlene (Robinson or Mitchell), 9) Piano, 10) Clifton

1) What was the name of the American ship discovered adrift and deserted in the Atlantic Ocean in 1872?

2) Which country has the longest coastline in the world?

3) On which golf course does the US masters take place every year?

4) Which part of the human body does 'pulmonary' relate to?

5) What are 'gambas' in Spain?

6) Which author wrote the Satanic Verses?

7) In 1997, Zaire became known as what?

8) Na'vi is a race of humanoids in which fictional film?

9) Which station in London is the busiest station in Europe by the volume of rail traffic?

10) What is the name of the leader of the wolf pack in the novel The Jungle Book and can also be the name used for the leader of a scout group?

Quiz 90 – Answers

1) Piccadilly line, 2) The Catcher in the Rye, 3) Ferdinand Magellan, 4) Blitzen, 5) Walker, 6) Notts County, 7) Marlene, 8) Bread, 9) Nine-ball pool, 10) Gone with the Wind, 1939

94

1) What was the name of the world's first operational nuclear-powered submarine?

2) Who narrated the War of the Worlds on radio in 1938, which became famous for allegedly causing mass panic when listeners supposedly believed it to be true?

3) In what year did India achieve independence?

4) What was the name of the British peer who disappeared in 1974 having been the suspect in a murder enquiry?

5) The Sykes–Picot Agreement was a secret agreement in 1916 between which two nations?

6) 'Glassnost' and 'Perestoika' were political movements and policy reform in which country?

7) Who was the Governor of the Bank of England before Mervyn King?

8) Francois Duvalier, ruler of Haiti, was also known by what other name?

9) Which tribe was Boudicca the leader of?

10) What was the nickname of William Joyce, the American born Nazi propaganda broadcaster to the UK during World War II?

Quiz 91 – Answers

1) Azerbaijan, 2) The Missouri River, 3) Hobart, 4) China and Pakistan, 5) Mexico, 6) Somalia, 7) Russia, 8) Indonesia, 9) Chihuahuan Desert, 10) Denver

1) What does the 'D.C' stand for in Washington D.C?

2) What was Operation Sea Lion?

3) Where is the 'home of golf'?

4) In which country was the Velvet revolution?

5) Which future king once competed at Wimbledon?

6) Who is generally credited with having invented the radio?

7) In which U.S state is Jack Daniels whiskey made?

8) Who originally wrote the song 'Hallelujah'?

9) The Gobi Desert is located in which two countries?

10) What is the lion called in the story of 'The lion, the Witch and the Wardrobe'?

Quiz 92 – Answers

1) The Mary Celeste, 2) Canada, 3) Augusta National Golf Club, 4) The lungs, 5) Prawns, 6) Salman Rushdie, 7) The Democratic Republic of Congo, 8) Avatar, 9) Clapham Junction, 10) Akela

Quiz 95 - Sport and Leisure

1) What is the name of the most successful sailor in Olympic history who won medals at five consecutive Olympics?

2) Which cricket umpire is known for his dramatic signalling style, which includes the famous "crooked finger of doom" 'Out' signal?

3) Which English footballer's nickname was 'Psycho'?

4) What is the national sport of Ireland?

5) In which two sports do men and women compete against each other head to head in the Olympics (excluding any mixed doubles events)?

6) Yorkshire Carnegie is a team that plays which sport?

7) What is the surname of the famous British violinist who also competed under the name of Vanessa Vanakorn for Thailand in alpine skiing at the 2014 Winter Olympics?

8) Who was the first ever £1million football player?

9) What is the maximum amount of time allowed to look for a lost ball in golf?

10) At the Rio Olympics in 2016, who became Team GB's oldest Olympic gold medallist for 108 years after winning the individual show jumping category?

Quiz 93 – Answers

1) USS Nautilus, 2) Orson Welles, 3) 1947, 4) Lord Lucan, 5) The UK and France, 6) USSR, 7) Eddie George, 8) Papa Doc, 9) Iceni, 10) Lord Haw-Haw

1) What was the name of the ship, which was at the time the world's largest passenger ship, and was sunk by a German submarine off the coast of Ireland during World War I, causing diplomatic outrage?

2) Which U.S state is named in honour of Elizabeth I?

3) How did Michael Schumacher sustain his life changing head injuries in 2013?

4) Who wrote the Wind in The Willows?

5) What does the mental disorder ADHD stand for?

6) With a name meaning 'The Red One', what is the name of the fortress and palace complex in Granada, Spain?

7) What was the name of Oscar Wilde's only novel?

8) Which of the US 'Great Lakes' is the largest?

9) Where did Captain Cook first land in Australia?

10) What is the name of the pub in Emmerdale?

Quiz 94 – Answers

1) District of Colombia, 2) Nazi Germany's plan for the invasion of England, 3) St. Andrews, 4) Czechoslovakia, 5) King George VI, 6) Guglielmo Marconi, 7) Tennessee, 8) Leonard Cohen, 9) Mongolia and China, 10) Aslan

Quiz 97 - Science and Nature

1) What is the alternative name for German measles?

2) What is the name of the constellation known for its easily recognizable distinctive 'W' shape, formed by five bright stars?

3) What is the fastest flying bird in the world?

4) What is the medical name for the shin bone?

5) What minimum number is a hurricane on the Beaufort scale?

6) What is a baby dolphin called?

7) The founder of the car brand Lamborghini originally made what type of vehicles?

8) What do you measure with a hygrometer?

9) What does SETI, the name of a long-standing scientific programme, stand for?

10) In any normal distribution, approximately what percentage of the data falls within two standard deviations of the mean?

Quiz 95 – Answers

1) Ben Ainslie, 2) Billy Bowden, 3) Stuart Pearce, 4) Hurling, 5) Equestrian events and Sailing, 6) Rugby Union, 7) Vanessa Mae, 8) Trevor Francis, 9) 5 minutes, 10) Nick Skelton

1) Eboracum was a fort city in Roman Britain on the site of which modern day city?

2) Which two colours are the names of the main tributaries of the river Nile?

3) The House of Lancaster kings all had what first name?

4) In 1985, which 17 year old became the first unseeded player to win the Men's Singles title at Wimbledon?

5) What is named using the Bayer designation system?

6) With a type of shoe named after it, what is the name of the line on a ship showing the legal limit to which a ship may be loaded?

7) In golf, what is the informal name given to nervous tension that commonly hinders putting?

8) Who or what was Herbie in the 1974 film `Herbie Rides Again`?

9) Which country produces the most gold in the world? (In 2017 this country produced over 40% more than its next closest competitor.)

10) Who created The Simpsons?

Quiz 96 – Answers

1) The Lusitania, 2) Virginia, 3) In a skiing accident, 4) Kenneth Grahame, 5) Attention deficit hyperactivity disorder, 6) The Alhambra, 7) The Picture of Dorian Gray, 8) Lake Superior, 9) Botany Bay, 10) The Woolpack

1) Which Iraqi born female architect, who died in 2016, designed buildings such as the London Aquatics Centre and Guangzhou Opera House?

2) Who played Voldemort in the Harry Potter films?

3) What is the name of the Mermaid princess in 'The little Mermaid' Disney film?

4) In the James Bond series of films, what is the name of 'M's' personal secretary?

5) In which American city was the TV show `Cheers` set?

6) Which Spanish novel by Miguel de Cervantes Saavedra, published in the 17th century, is considered one the most influential works of literature ever, and is also supposedly one of the highest selling books ever globally?

7) In the Lion King, Mufasa is Simba's father, Sarabi is his mother, but what is the name of his childhood friend and subsequent partner?

8) Brandon Flowers is the lead singer of which band?

9) What is the name of Superman's home planet?

10) Who played Captain Mainwaring in the sitcom Dad's Army?

Quiz 97 – Answers

1) Rubella, 2) Cassiopeia, 3) A Peregrine Falcon, 4) Tibia, 5) Twelve, 6) Calf, 7) Tractors, 8) Humidity, 9) Search for extra-terrestrial intelligence, 10) 95%

1) What is the name of the ship now on display in Greenwich, London, which is said to be the world's only surviving tea clipper, and was supposedly the fastest ship of her time?

2) What is the third tallest mountain in the world after Mount Everest and K2?

3) What was the name of the Soviet space dog that became the first animal to orbit the earth?

4) Name the orange properties on a standard monopoly board?

5) What was the surname of Eddie 'The Eagle'?

6) What is the nearest spiral galaxy to the Milky Way?

7) What does a costermonger sell?

8) The Crickets are which artist's backing band?

9) The Water of Leith is the main river running through which city?

10) Who wrote The Hitchhiker's Guide to the Galaxy?

Quiz 98 – Answers

1) York, 2) White Nile and Blue Nile, 3) Henry, 4) Boris Becker, 5) Stars, 6) Plimsoll line, 7) Yips, 8) A VW Beetle car, 9) China, 10) Matt Groening

1) Where is the 'Dome of the rock'?

2) What sea separates Australia and New Zealand?

3) Which is the largest city by population on the continent of Europe?

4) The Clifton Suspension Bridge spans which river?

5) The Gulf of Lion lies to the south of which country?

6) Antigua and Barbuda are part of which Caribbean island group?

7) How many stars are there on the US flag?

8) The Walloons are a race of people from which European country?

9) The river Aire runs through which UK city?

10) Which state joined the USA last, Hawaii or Alaska?

Quiz 99 – Answers

1) Zaha Hadid, 2) Ralph Fiennes, 3) Ariel, 4) Miss Moneypenny, 5) Boston, 6) Don Quixote, 7) Nala, 8) The Killers, 9) Krypton, 10) Arthur Lowe

1) In which city is Heriot-Watt University based?

2) What is Barack Obama's middle name?

3) Which tennis player was famously stabbed while on court in 1993?

4) What unit is defined as the energy to increase one gram of water by one degree Celsius?

5) What number is MCMXCIX?

6) What percentage of people are left handed?

7) Who wrote the erotic novel 'Fifty Shades Of Grey'?

8) Of the 50 busiest train stations in the world, all but five are said to be in which country?

9) Who was the founder of the Monster Raving Loony Party?

10) What is the famous pangram that is supposedly the shortest sentence containing every letter of the alphabet?

Quiz 100 – Answers

1) The Cutty Sark, 2) Kangchenjunga, 3) Laika, 4) Vine Street, Bow Street, Marlborough Street, 5) Edwards, 6) Andromeda, 7) Fruit and Veg, 8) Buddy Holly, 9) Edinburgh, 10) Douglas Adams

Quiz 103 - History and Politics

1) What was the name of the Kray twin's gang?

2) Which MP is known as 'The Beast of Bolsover'?

3) What was the commission that investigated the assassination of JFK most commonly known as?

4) Name either of the two places, (one in the Baltic and one in the Adriatic") that Winston Churchill said the 'Iron Curtain' was from and to?

5) Who was the first woman to take her seat as an MP in the House of Commons?

6) Who became the first Prime Minister of the State of Israel?

7) Who is the only US president to have never been elected?

8) Which British king was dethroned by the Glorious revolution?

9) What was the former name of the Russian city of Volgograd before its name was changed in 1961?

10) In what year was the 'Suez Crisis'?

Quiz 101 – Answers

1) Jerusalem, 2) The Tasman Sea, 3) Istanbul, 4) The River Avon, 5) France, 6) The Leeward Islands, 7) 50 (one for each state), 8) Belgium, 9) Leeds, 10) Hawaii

1) Which is the largest country in the world with only one time zone?

2) What did Adolph Sax invent?

3) What is the last letter of the Greek alphabet?

4) In which modern day country is the city of Troy?

5) What date of the month is the 'Ides of March'?

6) Who is the only runner ever to win the 5000 meters, 10000 meters and marathon in the same Olympics?

7) In which country was the radio mast that was the tallest structure in the world from 1974 until it collapsed in 1991?

8) What is 10 to the power 0?

9) What is the name of the 'complex' used by Sigmund Freud to describe a child's feelings of desire for his opposite-sex parent?

10) Which BBC TV show ran from 1964 to 2006?

Quiz 102 – Answers

1) Edinburgh, 2) Hussein, 3) Monica Seles, 4) Calorie, 5) 1999, 6) 10%, 7) E.L James, 8) Japan, 9) 'Screaming Lord Sutch' (David Such), 10) The quick brown fox jumps over a lazy dog

Quiz 105 - Sport and Leisure

1) What is the name for a delivery bowled in Cricket without any runs scored off it?

2) Which two English football teams compete in the dock yard derby?

3) Which Spanish city is famous for its annual bull run?

4) What is the name of a person who directs a racing boat?

5) How many clubs are you allowed in your bag during a round of golf?

6) When did England last host the Football World Cup?

7) Which four time Olympic medal winning British athlete became MP for Falmouth and Camborne?

8) What sporting event takes place every year at Flushing Meadows?

9) What was the sporting nickname of Eric Esch?

10) In athletics, what was the Triple Jump formerly called?

Quiz 103 – Answers

1) The Firm, 2) Dennis Skinner, 3) The Warren Commission, 4) Stettin and Trieste, 5) Nancy Astor, 6) David Ben Gurion, 7) Gerald Ford, 8) King James II of England, 9) Stalingrad, 10) 1956

Quiz 106 - General Knowledge

1) With regard to postal codes, what does 'ZIP code' stand for?

2) Which city supposedly would have been the new capital city of England if Adolf Hitler's German Army had have successfully invaded?

3) What is the name of the stick held by a music conductor?

4) The Island of Zanzibar belongs to which country?

5) Who was Queen for just nine days in 1553?

6) What is the RAF's motto?

7) Where is St George's Park, the FA's national football centre, and home of the England team?

8) What is 'Myopia'?

9) What date is St George's day?

10) What is the name of Elvis Presley's daughter?

Quiz 104 – Answers

1) China, 2) Saxophone, 3) Omega, 4) Turkey, 5) 15th, 6) Emil Zatopek, 7) Poland, 8) 1, 9) Oedipus complex, 10) Top Of The Pops

Quiz 107 – Science and Nature

1) What is the species 'Caribou' better known as in the UK?

2) The journal 'Lancet' is associated with which industry?

3) What is measured in Scoville Units?

4) What animals head does a Minotaur have?

5) Thrust SSC was the vehicle used by Andy Green to attain what record in 1997?

6) The word `cerebral` refers to which part of the body?

7) Vitamin C is also known as what?

8) What does Cc stand for, with regard to motor engines?

9) What does Dutch elm disease affect?

10) Solid carbon dioxide is known by what name?

Quiz 105 – Answers

1) Dot Ball, 2) Plymouth and Portsmouth, 3) Pamplona, 4) Coxswain, 5) 14, 6) 1966, 7) Seb Coe, 8) US Open in Tennis, 9) Butterbean, 10) Hop, Step and Jump

1) What is the phonetic alphabet word for 'O'?

2) In which Area of Outstanding Natural Beauty (AONB) is the source of the River Thames?

3) In which century was the Irish potato famine?

4) Which is the largest bone in the human body?

5) Which former England cricketer is nicknamed 'Beefy'?

6) Kublai Khan was emperor of which country?

7) What is the title of Ian Fleming's first James Bond novel?

8) Who is the only player to score a hat-trick in a World Cup final?

9) Pete Townshend, Roger Daltrey, Keith Moon and John Entwistle made up which band?

10) From which type of wood was Noah's Ark supposedly made from?

Quiz 106 – Answers

1) Zone Improvement Plan, 2) Oxford. He is said to have wanted Blenheim Palace as his residence, 3) Baton, 4) Tanzania, 5) Lady Jane Grey, 6) Per Ardua ad Astra (Through Adversity to the Stars), 7) Burton upon Trent, 8) Short-sightedness, 9) 23rd April, 10) Lisa Marie Presley

Quiz 109 – The Arts and Entertainment

1) What is the alternative pen name used by JK Rowling?

2) How are Conquest, War, Famine and Death collectively known in the Bible?

3) Which Welsh town is famous for its bookshops?

4) Soul singer Bobby Brown married which female singer?

5) What is the name of the French national anthem?

6) What is the name of the animated character in the computer game Tomb Raider?

7) What does UB stand for in the band name UB40?

8) Who wrote the opera Madama Butterfly?

9) In the Star Wars films, who killed Jabba the Hutt?

10) What is the name of Springfield's rival town in the Simpsons?

Quiz 107 – Answers

1) Reindeer, 2) Medical Industry, 3) The heat of chilli peppers/ spicy foods, 4) Bull, 5) The land speed record, 6) The brain, 7) Ascorbic acid, 8) Cubic Centimetres, 9) Trees, 10) Dry ice

1) Who was Elton John`s `Candle in the Wind` song originally written about?

2) What is the tallest building in the world?

3) What are the four main ingredients of a Waldorf salad?

4) What does the 'F' stand for in JFK?

5) Which city hosted the 2018 Winter Olympics?

6) What is the piece of plastic covering the tip of a shoelace called?

7) What is a formicary?

8) In which city was the RMS Titanic built?

9) What is the most commonly fractured bone in the human body?

10) Which quiz show is famous for the line `I`ve started so I`ll finish`?

Quiz 108 – Answers

1) Oscar, 2) The Cotswolds, 3) 19th, 4) Femur, 5) Ian Botham, 6) China, 7) Casino Royale, 8) Geoff Hurst, 9) The Who, 10) Gopher Wood

1) What is the second largest city in the Republic of Ireland, by population?

2) What is the biggest island in Europe?

3) The city of Las Vegas was named by the Spanish, but what does its name mean?

4) Where is the International Monetary Fund (IMF) based?

5) The Canary Islands are named after which animal?

6) A Scottish mountain must be at least how many feet high to be called a Munro?

7) What is the capital of the state of New York?

8) In which city is De Montfort University based?

9) What is the Currency of Vietnam?

10) The megalopolis 'Randstad', is made up of the four largest cities in which country?

Quiz 109 – Answers

1) Robert Galbrieth, 2) The Four Horsemen of the Apocalypse, 3) Hay-on-Wye, 4) Whitney Houston, 5) La Marseillaise, 6) Lara Croft, 7) Unemployment Benefit, 8) Giacomo Puccini, 9) Princess Leia, 10) Shelbyville

Quiz 112 – General Knowledge

1) 'Ayers Rock' in Australia, is known locally under what name?

2) If you have two dimes and three nickels, how many cents do you have?

3) Who performed the title song for the James Bond movie Die Another Day?

4) What is the name of the former professional boxer who has also served as a Senator of the Philippines?

5) What are members of The Church of Jesus Christ of Latter-day Saints more commonly known as?

6) Which breed of cat has no tail?

7) What does the bank HSBC's name stand for?

8) What name is given to a word that is spelt the same backwards?

9) In which street did the great fire of London start?

10) Name either of the co-founders of Wikipedia?

Quiz 110 – Answers

1) Marilyn Monroe, 2) Burj Khalifa, Dubai, 3) Apples, celery, walnuts, grapes, 4) Fitzgerald, 5) Pyeongchang, 6) An aglet, 7) An ant colony - a pile of earth where ants live, 8) Belfast, 9)The clavicle (collar bone), 10) Mastermind

1) Put these three major wartime conferences in chronological order; Potsdam, Tehran, Yalta.

2) Name either of the two US presidents who were impeached.

3) In what type of venue was Abraham Lincoln assassinated?

4) After his abdication, Edward VIII took what title?

5) What is the name of the formula used by the UK treasury to adjust the amounts of public spending allocated to Scotland, Wales and Northern Ireland?

6) What was the name of the Sherpa who accompanied Edmund Hillary to the summit of Mount Everest?

7) What is the name of the Israeli parliament?

8) Who was the founder of the country of North Korea in 1948?

9) What is the name of the Indian city where the world's worst ever industrial accident occurred in 1984?

10) What is the name of the Vietnamese revolutionary leader, who now also has a city in Vietnam named after him?

Quiz 111 – Answers

1) Cork, 2) Great Britain, 3) The Meadows, 4) Washington, D.C, 5) Dogs (derived from Latin for dogs, and not canaries, who are named after the islands) , 6) 3000, 7) Albany, 8) Leicester, 9) The Vietnamese dong, 10) The Netherlands (Amsterdam, Rotterdam, The Hague, and Utrecht)

1) What brand of beer does Homer Simpson drink?

2) The island of Svalbard is in which ocean?

3) If you have an immune reaction and intolerance to Gluten, what disease are you said to have?

4) What is the name of the site of Northern Ireland's main government buildings, including the Northern Ireland Assembly?

5) In what decade was the last moonwalk?

6) Between the Moscow and Seoul Olympics, where were they hosted?

7) How long does it take for light from the Sun to reach the Earth in whole minutes?

8) What building is pictured on a bottle of HP sauce?

9) Who had a hit in 1984 with `99 Red Balloons`?

10) Since 1977, the World Snooker Championship has been played at the Crucible Theatre in which city?

Quiz 112 – Answers

1) Uluru, 2) 35, 3) Madonna, 4) Manny Pacquiao, 5) Mormons, 6) Manx cat, 7) Hong Kong and Shanghai Banking Corporation, 8) Palindrome, 9) Pudding Lane, 10) Jimmy Wales and Larry Sanger

Quiz 115 – Sport and Leisure

1) What is the name for the mathematical formula used to calculate the target score for the team batting second in a limited overs cricket match which has been interrupted most commonly by weather?

2) Who was first foreign manager of the England Men's National Football team?

3) Which sport is played on a court that is 18 meters (59 feet) long and 9 meters (29.5 feet) wide?

4) How many gold medals did Jesse Owens win at the 1936 Olympics?

5) Near which bridge does the University boat race start?

6) What is the highest number in bingo?

7) Who famously shouted at a Wimbledon umpire "You cannot be serious!" and "You are the pits of the world!"?

8) As of 2020, how many points does the winner of a Formula 1 race receive?

9) In which city is the 'Bird's Nest Stadium'?

10) As of 2020, how many different teams have ever played in the English Premier League, 30-50, 50-60, or more than 60?

Quiz 113 – Answers

1)Tehran, Yalta, Potsdam, 2) Andrew Johnson and Bill Clinton, 3) Theatre, 4) Duke of Windsor, 5) Barnett Formula, 6) Tenzing Norgay, 7) The Knesset, 8) Kim Il-Sung, 9) Bhopal, 10) Ho Chi Minh

1) What is the Japanese art-form of paper folding called?

2) The play `Pygmalion` was adapted to become which musical?

3) Who was the Roman god of love?

4) What does the term Bcc stand for when sending an email?

5) What was the famous darts player Eric Bristow's nickname?

6) What is the name of the famous bell that hangs in the underwriting room in Lloyd's of London?

7) What is the opposite of the word 'oriental'?

8) What is the name of Queen Victoria's former residence on the Isle of Wight?

9) What is the angle between the hands of a clock at 1 o'clock?

10) Who played the character Melchett in the Blackadder sitcom?

Quiz 114 – Answers

1) Duff Beer, 2) Arctic Ocean, 3) Celiac disease, 4) Stormont, 5) 70's (1972), 6) Los Angeles (1984), 7) 8, 8) The Houses of Parliament, 9) Nena, 10) Sheffield

1) What do you call a male duck?

2) Who created the principles of Demand and Supply in the field of Economics?

3) What does NASA stand for?

4) What is the chemical symbol for Mercury?

5) By what name is the Chinese gooseberry more commonly known?

6) Which group of animal's name means terrible or fearfully great lizard in ancient Greek?

7) What SI unit is radioactivity measured in?

8) Hepatitis affects which part of the human body?

9) What is Jodrell Bank?

10) What is the name for a group of cats?

1) Duckworth Lewis, 2) Sven-Göran Eriksson, 3) Volleyball, 4) 4, 5) Putney Bridge, 6) 90, 7) John McEnroe, 8) 25, 9) Beijing, 10) 30-50 (49 to be exact)

1) The islands of Mauritius are in which ocean?

2) What famous natural event happened in 1883, causing the deaths of thousands of people?

3) From which country is the manufacturer of Skoda cars?

4) What are the terms 'Potus' and 'Flotus' referring to?

5) Which country did boxer Lennox Lewis represent at the Olympics?

6) In what year was the Chernobyl accident?

7) How many lines does a sonnet have?

8) What was the name of the Austrian skydiver who jumped to earth from a helium balloon in the stratosphere in 2012, becoming the first person to break the sound barrier without vehicular power?

9) With regard to the international organisation, what do the initials NATO stand for?

10) Which country did Paddington bear come from?

Quiz 116 – Answers

1) Origami, 2) My Fair Lady, 3) Cupid, 4) Blind Carbon Copy, 5) The Crafty Cockney, 6) Lutine Bell, 7) Occidental, 8) Osbourne House, 9) 30 degrees, 10) Stephen Fry

1) Who sang the hit song 'Gangnam Style'?

2) Who was the Bard of Ayrshire?

3) Who wrote the novel 'War and Peace'?

4) Which single is widely thought to be the biggest selling single for a female group of all time?

5) Who played the character of Will, who was Ross' high school friend in the sitcom Friends?

6) What does QI stand for in the comedy TV show?

7) What was the Bronte sisters' brother called?

8) What is the name of the dot over the letters "i" and "j" called?

9) In which village is Fireman Sam set?

10) Who was the 'prisoner of Azkaban'?

Quiz 117 – Answers

1) A drake, 2) Alfred Marshall, 3) The National Aeronautics and Space Administration, 4) Hg, 5) Kiwi fruit, 6) Dinosaur, 7) Becquerels, 8) The liver, 9) An observatory, 10) A clowder

1) Who founded the internet company Amazon?

2) Which is taller, Snowdon, (the tallest mountain in Wales), or Scarfell Pike, (the tallest mountain in England)?

3) Where was Francis Drake supposedly playing bowls when he was warned that the Spanish Armada was coming?

4) What do the French call the English Channel?

5) What is the only object thrown in the woman's heptathlon?

6) What is the name of the fashion consultant who hosted the TV show 'How To Look Good Naked'?

7) Which country is Stollen from?

8) What is the closest star to planet earth other than the sun?

9) What date is Burns Night?

10) What was the name of the son of A.A Milne, the author of Winnie the Pooh?

Quiz 118 – Answers

1) Indian Ocean, 2) Eruption of Krakatoa, 3) Czech republic, 4) President of the United States and First Lady of the United States, 5) Canada, 6) 1986, 7) 14, 8) Felix Baumgartner, 9) North Atlantic Treaty Organisation, 10) Peru

1) Which UK city is also known as the Granite City?

2) Easter Island is a dependency of which country?

3) What is the name of the lake in the middle of Hyde Park?

4) Kampuchea is a former name of which modern day country?

5) Which county was Huntingdonshire absorbed into?

6) What is the capital of the state of Florida?

7) What is the driest non-polar desert in the world?

8) Name either of the two islands separating the Niagara Falls?

9) Venice gondolas, due to an old law, are customarily painted which colour?

10) In which province of Ireland is Dublin?

Quiz 119 – Answers

1) Psy, 2) Robert Burns, 3) Leo Tolstoy, 4) 'Wannabe', (The Spice Girls), 5) Brad Pitt, 6) Quite Interesting, 7) Branwell, 8) A tittle, 9) Pontypandy, 10) Sirius Black (In the Harry Potter series)

Quiz 122 – General Knowledge

1) Does biannual mean once every two years or twice a year?

2) Name the five boroughs of New York City?

3) Who supposedly gave King Arthur his sword?

4) What is the basic ingredient for the drink Calvados?

5) Name the four tennis Grand Slams?

6) There are two countries that have a native population of alligators. The US is one, what is the other?

7) By what other name might a 'Syrah' wine be known?

8) What is the name of the female singer-songwriter who died by being hit by speedboat while on holiday in Mexico in 2000?

9) In which palace was Winston Churchill born?

10) According to one of Aesop's fables, who took the thorn out of the lions paw?

Quiz 120 – Answers

1) Jeff Bezos, 2) Snowdon, 3) Plymouth Hoe, 4) La Manche, 5) Javelin, 6) Gok Wan, 7) Germany, 8) Proxima Centuri, 9) 25th January, 10) Christopher Robin

Quiz 123 – History and Politics

1) When was the Act of Union signed, which merged the Kingdoms of England and Scotland?

2) What are teenagers Eric Harris and Dylan Klebold infamous for?

3) Who sentenced Jesus to crucifixion?

4) In which country are the Tamil Tigers a separatist movement?

5) Who was first Roman emperor?

6) In Greek legend, who turned everything he touched into gold?

7) What was the name of the US army General who led the coalition forces in the Gulf War, and was nicknamed 'Stormin' Norman'?

8) In what year were the student demonstrations and protests in Tiananmen Square, Beijing?

9) What was the name of the legendary Benedictine monk who made important contributions to the production and quality of champagne wine in the 17th and 18th century?

10) What was the first name of Winston Churchill's wife?

Quiz 121 – Answers

1) Aberdeen, 2) Chile, 3) The Serpentine, 4) Cambodia, 5) Cambridgeshire, 6) Tallahassee, 7) The Atacama Desert, 8) Goat Island and Luna Island, 9) Black, 10) Leinster

Quiz 124 – General Knowledge

1) What is the capital of North Korea?

2) What are you said to be able to eat only when where there is an 'R' in the month?

3) Sharon Tate was murdered by members of a commune led by whom?

4) What is the UK area telephone dialling code for Manchester?

5) What is significant about Agüero, Defoe, Berbatov, Shearer and Cole?

6) What are Shahada (Faith), Salah (Prayer), Zakat (Charity), Sawm (Fasting) and Hajj (pilgrimage) collectively known as?

7) What is the fastest (bipedal) animal on two legs?

8) On what island is Thunderbirds set?

9) What is the alternative name for the purple flower 'digitalis'?

10) What is the national sport of the USA?

Quiz 122 – Answers

1) Twice a year, 2) Manhattan, Staten Island, Bronx, Brooklyn, Queens, 3) The Lady of the Lake, 4) lApples, 5) Australian Open, French Open, US Open, Wimbledon, 6) China, 7) Shiraz, 8) Kirsty MacColl, 9) Blenheim Palace, 10) Androcles

Quiz 125 – Sport and Leisure

1) Involving which two countries, and in which sport, was the first official international sports game played?

2) How far away from the goal is the penalty spot in football?

3) In snooker, which colour ball is in the centre of the table at the beginning of a game?

4) How many different coloured jerseys are awarded during the Tour De France?

5) How many times have the summer Olympic Games been cancelled due to war?

6) Which jockey famously rode all 7 winners on the card at a race meeting in Ascot in 1996?

7) What was the last year that England failed to qualify for a FIFA World Cup?

8) What was the name of the opponent who Mike Tyson bit the ear of during a fight?

9) Nicknamed 'Mighty Mike', who is the youngest ever winner of the PDC darts World Championship?

10) What event did Denise Lewis specialise in?

Quiz 123 – Answers

1) 1707, 2) The Columbine High School massacre, 3) Pontius Pilate, 4) Sri Lanka, 5) Augustus, 6) King Midas, 7) Norman Schwarzkopf, 8) 1989, 9) Dom Perignon, 10) Clementine

1) Vaduz is the capital of which country?

2) How long did the Hundred Years War last; 95 years, 108 years, or 116 years?

3) What is the name of the sport which generally comprises the events of tie-down roping, saddle bronc riding, bareback bronc riding, and barrel racing, amongst others?

4) Renal, refers to which part of the body?

5) Johnny Rotten is the lead singer of which band?

6) In what year was the NHS formed in England?

7) To be a true Cockney, where specifically must you be born?

8) What major sporting event took place in 1930 for the first time?

9) Which wedding anniversary is represented by a gift of China?

10) Casino Royale was the first James Bond Novel, but what was the first James Bond film?

Quiz 124 – Answers

1) Pyongyang, 2) Oysters, 3) Charles Manson, 4) 0161, 5) They are the only players to have scored five goals in a Premier League game, 6) The five pillars of Islam, 7) Ostrich, 8) Tracey Island, 9) Foxglove, 10) Baseball

1) Who invented waterproof fabric and therefore has a type of coat named after him?

2) What was also known as the Carrington event?

3) How many pounds are in a British long hundredweight?

4) How many primary colours are there and can you name them?

5) By what name is the plant Belladonna more commonly known as?

6) What is the name of the figure of eight dance movement of honeybees to inform others about the direction of food?

7) Who is said to have run through the streets naked shouting "Eureka!"?

8) What is an epistaxis?

9) From which country is the astronomer and mathematician Nicolaus Copernicus?

10) What is someone who shoes horses called?

Quiz 125 – Answers

1) Cricket; USA vs Canada, 2) Twelve yards, 3) Blue, 4) Four; Yellow, Green, Polka Dot and White, 5) three times, 6) Frankie Dettori, 7) 1994, 8) Evander Holyfield, 9) Michael Van Gerwan, 10) Heptathlon

1) What pet did Lord Byron keep at Trinity College Cambridge after they wouldn't let him keep a dog?

2) What is measured with an anemometer?

3) Svetlana Alliluyeva defected from the USSR to become a citizen of the United States in 1967. Whose daughter was she?

4) What mountain range forms part of the continental boundary between Europe and Asia?

5) What number was on the back of the shirt that David Beckham wore while playing for Real Madrid?

6) On the tenth day of Christmas what did my true love give to me?

7) Who created the character Peter Pan?

8) On which island was Nelson Mandela imprisoned for 27 years?

9) What was the first ever 'Carry On...' film?

10) Which architect designed La Sagrada Família, the large unfinished Roman Catholic Church in Barcelona?

Quiz 126 – Answers

1) Liechtenstein, 2) 116 years, 3) Rodeo, 4) Kidneys, 5) The Sex Pistols, 6) 1948, 7) Within earshot of Bow bells, 8) Football World Cup, 9) 20th Anniversary, 10) Dr No

1) 'Slash' is the lead guitarist for which band?

2) In the novel of the same name, what is 'Wuthering Heights'?

3) As of 1999, a fixed term was introduced for the British Poet Laureate. How long is the term?

4) Who played Austin Powers in the film series?

5) Who painted the famous painting The Monarch of the Glen?

6) What was the occupation of Charlene Robinson, the character played by Kylie Minogue in the soap Neighbours?

7) Fill in the missing novel title in the Hunger Games trilogy: The Hunger Games, [.....], Mockingjay.

8) What is the name of the music festival in New York State which attracted over 400,000 people in 1969?

9) Referring to the American family comedy act, name the five Marx Brothers?

10) On what Island is Father Ted set?

Quiz 127 – Answers

1) Charles Macintosh, 2) A solar storm in 1859, one of the largest geomagnetic storms on record, 3) 112 pounds, 4) Three; Red, Yellow, Blue, 5) Deadly Nightshade, 6) Waggle dance, 7) Archimedes, 8) A nosebleed, 9) Poland, 10) A Farrier

1) What is a taikonaut?

2) The New Shekel is the currency of which country?

3) Fill in the missing UK Prime Minister: Wilson, [.....], Thatcher, Major.

4) Which two football clubs play in the 'Old Firm Derby'?

5) What are the two main ingredients of a Dark 'N' stormy cocktail?

6) In which decade was Channel 4 launched?

7) Which specific Olympic event do women perform to music yet men don't?

8) Who wrote the original 1964 novel 'Chitty-Chitty-Bang-Bang: The Magical car' which was subsequently made into a fantasy film written by Roald Dahl?

9) What did the 13th amendment to the US constitution do?

10) Who sang the hit rock and roll single in 1955 'Rock Around the Clock Tonight'?

Quiz 128 – Answers

1) A bear, 2) Wind Speed, 3) Joseph Stalin's, 4) The Urals, 5) 23, 6) Ten Lords a-leaping, 7) J.M Barrie, 8) Robben Island, 9) Carry on Sergeant, 10) Antoni Gaudí

Quiz 131 – Geography

1) In which Indian city is the Taj Mahal?

2) In 1917 from which country did the USA buy the now named United States Virgin Islands from?

3) Which set of hills is Cheddar Gorge situated in?

4) What is the name of the sea off the western coast of mainland Italy, east of the islands of Corsica and Sardinia and north of Sicily?

5) What is the name of the major river running through the city of Glasgow?

6) The city of Brisbane is in which Australian state?

7) Which London tube line goes from Brixton to Walthamstow Central?

8) What is the formerly named Sears tower in Chicago now officially known as?

9) What was the capital of ancient Egypt?

10) What did Spain cede to Britain in exchange for the return of Havana?

Quiz 129 – Answers

1) Guns 'N' Roses, 2) A house (Mr Heathcliff's dwelling), 3) Ten years, 4) Mike Myers, 5) Edwin Landseer, 6) A mechanic, 7) Catching Fire, 8) Woodstock, 9) Chico, Harpo, Groucho, Gummo, and Zeppo, 10) Craggy Island

1) What is the word 'cello', the stringed instrument, short for?

2) Mount Kosciuszko is the tallest mountain in which country?

3) What does the Audi company slogan 'Vorsprung durch Technik' mean?

4) In 1931, US president Hoover suggested that individuals should turn off their lights for one minute as a mark of respect upon the death of which person?

5) The football club R.S.C Anderlecht is based in which city?

6) What is the moon doing when it's 'waxing'?

7) George Galloway was the leader of which politic party?

8) What is the name of the fictional newspaper in the Superman comics?

9) What is the name of the drug used mostly to treat nausea in pregnant women, which caused thousands of women to give birth to disabled babies in the late 1950's and 1960's?

10) What is the name of the art of clipping trees and hedges into ornamental shapes?

Quiz 130 – Answers

1) A Chinese astronaut/ An astronaut from the Chinese Space Program, 2) Israel, 3) Callaghan, 4) Glasgow Rangers and Celtic, 5) Rum and ginger beer, 6) 1980s, 7) The Floor (in gymnastics), 8) Ian Fleming (The author of the James Bond novel series), 9) Abolished slavery, 10) Bill Haley and His Comets

1) What is Captain Edward Smith infamous for?

2) Eleanor of Aquitaine was married to which King of England?

3) The Battle of Goose Green was part of which war?

4) What is the name of the village near the de facto border of North and South Korea where the 1953 armistice was signed which halted the Korean War?

5) Also the name of a world famous band, what was the name of the type of plane used as a spy plane by the USA, one of which was shot down over the Soviet Union in 1960?

6) Who was the first leader of the Labour party?

7) In which country was Milton Obote overthrown as leader?

8) Name either of the Moors murderers of the 1960's?

9) The Five Star Movement is a political party in which country?

10) Who became the first female leader of Plaid Cymru?

Quiz 131 – Answers

1) Agra, 2) Denmark, 3) The Mendip Hills, 4) Tyrrhenian Sea, 5) The River Clyde, 6) Queensland, 7) Victoria line, 8) The Willis Tower, 9) Memphis, 10) Florida

1) What is the term used for the mythological 'city of gold' in South America?

2) On which day of the week is Maundy money given out?

3) In which city was US President JFK assassinated?

4) How many players is the maximum allowed in a scrum in Rugby Union?

5) Who was the President of the National union of Miners at the time of the miner's strikes in the 1980s?

6) Who wrote the science fiction novel 'The War of the Worlds'?

7) Name any of the events of a modern pentathlon?

8) It is estimated that the world population hit one billion around 1800. As of 2018, the current population is estimated to be 7.5 billion. How many people are estimated to have ever lived on the planet? A) 50-60 billion, B) 80-90 billion, or C) 100-110 billion?

9) What is a funambulist?

10) Who is the keeper of the ring in The Lord of the Rings?

Quiz 132 – Answers

1) Violoncello, 2) Australia, 3) Being ahead through technology, 4) Thomas Edison (Inventor of the lightbulb), 5) Brussels, 6) Going from new moon to full moon (or getting larger in sight), 7) Respect Party, 8) The Daily Planet, 9) Thalidomide, 10) Topiary

1) Ex England manager Steve McClaren has managed two teams abroad, can you name either of them?

2) In Monopoly, what is the cost of Old Kent Road?

3) From which wood is a cricket bat traditionally made from?

4) How many jumps are there in the Grand National race?

5) Where is the Mulsanne straight?

6) At the end of which season was the English Premier League reduced to 20 teams from 22?

7) In which sport are you banned from playing left handed due to safety reasons?

8) In which park was the first ever 'parkrun' ran?

9) Which sport uses the lightest ball?

10) In which sport is the Egg position used?

Quiz 133 – Answers

1) He was Captain of the RMS Titanic, 2) Henry II, 3) The Falklands War, 4) Panmunjom, 5) U-2, 6) Keir Hardie, 7) Uganda, 8) Ian Brady and Myra Hindley, 9) Italy, 10) Leanne Wood

Quiz 136 – General Knowledge

1) The building at 30, St Mary's Axe, London, is better known by what name?

2) Timothy McVeigh was executed in the US in 2001 for committing which crime?

3) In Greek mythology, what are the names of the twins of Gemini?

4) What is the name of the curved sword associated with sailors and pirates?

5) Which is the biggest size of bottle; a jeroboam, a methuselah or a Balthazar?

6) What was Judas' surname in the Bible?

7) Brazil has borders with every single other South American country, except which two?

8) Which film won eleven Oscars in 1959?

9) Who was the first DJ to broadcast on Radio 1?

10) Which children's book series did Roger Hargreaves author?

Quiz 134 – Answers

1) El Dorado, 2) Thursday (the day before Good Friday), 3) Dallas, 4) 8, 5) Arthur Scargill, 6) H. G. Wells, 7) Freestyle Swimming, Fencing, Equestrian Show Jumping, Pistol Shooting, Cross Country Running, 8) C) 100-110 billion. (Estimated at 107 billion), 9) A tightrope walker, 10) Frodo

Quiz 137 – Science and Nature

1) What is the name for a person who studies or collects butterflies and moths?

2) What does 'DNA' stand for?

3) What is the pH number of pure water?

4) Haematology is the study of what?

5) The offspring of which two animals is called a mule?

6) What is the lemniscate symbol used to represent in mathematics?

7) What is the closest layer of the atmosphere to the earth?

8) What was bovine spongiform encephalopathy more informally known as?

9) What is the largest moon in our solar system?

10) What is the chemical symbol for Silver?

Quiz 135 – Answers

1) Twente, VfL Wolfsburg, 2) £60, 3) Willow, 4) 30 (16 different ones, 14 of which are jumped twice), 5) Circuit de la Sarthe/ Le Mans (part of the Le Mans 24 hour race), 6) 1994-95, 7) Polo, 8) Bushy Park, London, 9) Table Tennis, 10) Skiing

Quiz 138 – General Knowledge

1) In which U.S state is the city of Seattle in?

2) What is the common name for the nautical signal flag representing the letter 'P', which means that a ship is about to proceed to sea?

3) If you were served 'escargots' in France, what would you be eating?

4) In Greek mythology, what was the name of the female monster that had snakes for hair and turned people who stared at her into stone?

5) Who is the only ever UK Prime Minister to speak English as a second language?

6) In medicine, what does CPR stand for?

7) Which of the following boxing classes is the heaviest - flyweight, bantam weight or feather weight?

8) Which establishment has the motto "Nation Shall Speak Peace Unto Nation"?

9) Who authored The Jungle Book?

10) What does the graduate degree MBA stand for?

Quiz 136 – Answers

1) The Gherkin, 2) The 1995 Oklahoma City bombings, 3) Castor and Pollux, 4) A cutlass, 5) Balthazar, 6) Iscariot, 7) Ecuador and Chile, 8) Ben Hur, 9) Tony Blackburn, 10) Mr Men series

Quiz 139 – The Arts and Entertainment

1) Who wrote the book 'Gulliver's Travels', which was first published in 1726?

2) Who played 'Trigger' in the sitcom Only Fools and Horses?

3) Which superhero's alter ego is James "Logan" Howlett?

4) What is E. M. Forster's first name?

5) In which police station was 'The Bill' set?

6) What type of hat did Sherlock Holmes wear?

7) As of 2020, what is the most expensive movie ever produced?

8) Which American novelist, who won the Nobel Prize for Literature in 1954, wrote 'The Old Man and the Sea' and 'For Whom the Bell Tolls'?

9) Command station, this is ST321, code clearance blue" is the opening line of which film?

10) Who was the best-selling recording artist from 1939 to 1943 who disappeared in a plane over the English Channel while he was traveling to entertain U.S. troops in France during World War II?

Quiz 137 – Answers

1) Lepidopterist, 2) Deoxyribonucleic acid, 3) 7, 4) Blood, 5) Donkey and horse, 6) Infinity, 7) Troposphere, 8) Mad cow disease, 9) Ganymede, 10) Ag

1) Which famous dam is situated on the River Nile?

2) How many litres in a gallon (to one decimal place)?

3) In which country was the Mau Mau rebellion in the 1950's and 60's?

4) If you 'step up to the plate', which sport are you playing?

5) Commonly used in furniture, what do the initials MDF stand for?

6) In what year did hurricane Katrina destroy large parts of New Orleans as well as other parts of Louisiana and Florida?

7) How many semitones are there in an octave?

8) According to the Bible, what is God said to have created on the second day of creation?

9) What was the name of Argentine cruiser sunk by a Royal Navy submarine during the Falkland war?

10) Ali Baba is associated with how many thieves in the name of the folk tale?

Quiz 138 – Answers

1) Washington, 2) Blue Peter, 3) Snails, 4) Medusa, 5) David Lloyd George (Welsh was his first language), 6) Cardiopulmonary Resuscitation, 7) Feather weight, 8) The BBC, 9) Rudyard Kipling, 10) Master of Business Administration

1) By volume, which is the world's largest freshwater lake?

2) What is the second largest city in Egypt after Cairo?

3) What is the capital of the Falkland Islands?

4) What is the old country of British Honduras now known as?

5) Which four British cities have underground rail systems?

6) The Indian state of Goa used to be a colony of which country?

7) On which island is there a city called Larnaca?

8) In which country is the impact crater from an asteroid which is widely thought to be the cause of the extinction of the dinosaurs?

9) What is the largest dam in the world?

10) To which town in France do people make a pilgrimage to, due to a faith in miraculous cures being possible there?

Quiz 139 – Answers

1) Jonathon Swift, 2) Roger Lloyd Pack, 3) Wolverine, 4) Edward, 5) Sun Hill Police Station, 6) A deerstalker, 7) Pirates of the Caribbean: On Stranger Tides, 8) Ernest Hemingway, 9) Return of the Jedi, 10) Glenn Miller

143

1) Which type of animal marries the Owl and the Pussycat in the Edward Lear poem?

2) Which constellation features on the flags of five different nations, including both New Zealand and Australia?

3) In which country might you pay for something using Kopeks?

4) Which politician was nicknamed 'Two Jags' by the British media?

5) What is the name of the art of reading tea leaves called?

6) There are five nations that have competed in every single modern Olympic Games, name 3 of them.

7) In what year was the 'Boxing Day tsunamis' that killed over 225,000 people across an incredible 14 countries?

8) What is the name of the Irish playwright who wrote Pygmalion, first published in 1913?

9) What is the southernmost capital city in the world?

10) What is the name of the painting by Rene Magritte that depicts a man standing whose face is obscured from view by an apple?

Quiz 140 – Answers

1) Aswan Dam or Aswan High Dam, 2) 4.5, 3) Kenya, 4) Baseball, 5) Medium-density Fibreboard, 6) 2005, 7) Twelve, 8) The sky, 9) The ARA General Belgrano or commonly 'The Belgrano', 10) 40

1) Fill in the gap to complete the names of the Russian city over the years: St Petersburg, [...] Leningrad, St Petersburg.

2) Which two other countries joined the EEC in the same year as the UK?

3) Also the leader of the DUP, who became the first ever female First Minister of Northern Ireland when she was elected in 2016?

4) The Jacobean era relates to which monarch?

5) What was the surname of the president of Egypt who ordered the seizing of the Suez Canal, causing the Suez Crisis of the 1950's?

6) What date was D-Day?

7) Who led The Charge of the Light Brigade?

8) The only ever English pope took which name?

9) William booth founded which army?

10) Ptolemy XV Philopator Philometor Caesar, better known by the nickname Caesarion, was the last Pharaoh of Egypt and the son of which two famous people?

Quiz 141 – Answers

1) Lake Baikal, 2) Alexandria, 3) Port Stanley, 4) Belize, 5) Liverpool, Glasgow, Newcastle and London, 6) Portugal, 7) Cyprus, 8) Mexico, 9) Three Gorges Dam, 10) Lourdes

1) On which island is the nation of Brunei?

2) In what year was Queen Elizabeth II crowned?

3) According to tradition, if it rains on a certain bridge in Winchester on the 15th July it will continue for 40 days. What is the name of this bridge, which is named after a Saint?

4) How many more players are in a rugby union team than a rugby league team?

5) A sardine is the young of which fish?

6) Who played Manuel in `Fawlty Towers`?

7) In what decade was the last person to be hanged in the UK for committing a crime?

8) In which region of Portugal was Cristiano Ronaldo born? The place also has a famous toboggan run.

9) The sitcom Frasier, is a spin-off of which series?

10) Which author's only novel was Wuthering heights?

Quiz 142 – Answers

1) A Turkey, 2) The Southern Cross, 3) Russia, 4) John Prescott, 5) Tasseography, 6) Australia, Greece, France, Great Britain, Switzerland, 7) 2004, 8) George Bernard Shaw, 9) Wellington (New Zealand), 10) The son of man

1) Fill in the missing Premier League winning team: Manchester City, Chelsea, [.....], Chelsea, Manchester City.

2) Which British middle distance athlete was nicknamed the 'Jarrow Arrow'?

3) What do the initials 'TT' stand for in the Isle of Man race?

4) Who was the last British woman to win a tennis Grand Slam tournament?

5) Situated in Newmarket, what is the name of the main race horse auctioneer in the UK?

6) Which two events make up a Biathalon?

7) What is 'BMX' short for?

8) When was the last time the Winter and Summer Olympics were held in the same year?

9) In which stadium did 39 people (mostly Juventus fans) die at a European Cup final football game against Liverpool for which English clubs served a five year European competition ban?

10) The famous actor Jason Statham competed for England at the 1990 Commonwealth Games in which sport?

Quiz 143 – Answers

1) Petrograd, 2) Denmark and the Republic of Ireland, 3) Arlene Foster, 4) James I of England (James VI of Scotland), 5) Nasser (Gamal Abdel), 6) 6th June 1944, 7) Lord Cardigan, 8) Pope Adrian IV, 9) The Salvation Army, 10) Cleopatra and Julius Caesar

1) What is Inspector Morse's first name?

2) What are the canals in Cambridge called?

3) What did the Acts of Supremacy do?

4) What is Japanese for 'person of art', and is the name of a woman who entertains men with music and dance?

5) Who was the king of the Roman gods, equivalent to the Greek god Zeus?

6) The Calcutta Cup is awarded after a certain game between England and Scotland in which sport?

7) Which animals live in an Apiary?

8) What is the name of the novel which Joseph Heller is most famous for?

9) What was the name of the Norwegian who killed 69 people in a terrorist attack on Utøya island in 2011?

10) What was the name of the orphaned boy in The Jungle book?

Quiz 144 – Answers

1) Borneo, 2) 1953, 3) St Swithin's bridge, 4) Two more. 13 in a rugby league team, 15 in a rugby union team, 5) A Pilchard, 6) Andrew Sachs, 7) 1960s, 8) Madeira, 9) Cheers, 10) Emily Brontë

1) What do you call the kitchen area of a boat, ship or aircraft?

2) Where are your phalanges?

3) What is the chemical symbol for table salt?

4) Which is the main protein in milk?

5) What are the first three letters on the left hand side of the bottom row of a standard computer keyboard?

6) What type of paper is used to test whether a liquid is an acid or alkali?

7) The ABO grouping system classifies what?

8) If you multiply the diameter of a tube by two, by how many times has its capacity increased?

9) What are the computer initials USB abbreviated from?

10) What is the study of animals called?

Quiz 145 – Answers

1) Leicester City (2016), 2) Steve Cram, 3) Tourist Trophy, 4) Virginia Wade, 5) Tattersalls, 6) Cross Country Skiing and Rifle Shooting, 7) bicycle motocross, 8) 1992, 9) Heysel Stadium, 10) Diving

1) Who flew the Spirit of St Louis in the first solo non-stop transatlantic flight?

2) What does NME stand for, with regard to the music journalism website and former magazine that has been published since 1952?

3) Where was the original capital of Roman Britain?

4) What is the name of Tintin's companion dog in the comic series?

5) What is the name of the ornament on the bonnet of a Rolls Royce car? It is in the form of a woman leaning forwards with her arms outstretched behind her.

6) Originally, what item would a saboteur use?

7) What was Al Capone's job, according to his business card?

8) By what name is Marshal Mathers more commonly known?

9) Speleology is the study of what?

10) Which two brothers wrote fairy tales including Rapunzel, Rumpelstiltskin, and Hansel and Grethel?

Quiz 146 – Answers

1) Endeavour, 2) The Backs, 3) Made Henry VIII the supreme head of the Church of England, 4) 'Geisha' (girl), 5) Jupiter,6) Rugby Union, 7) Bees, 8) Catch-22, 9) Anders Breivik, 10) Mowgli

1) Who wrote the fictional children's series featuring the character Noddy?

2) From which country does the band A-Ha come from?

3) Who wrote the 2001 novel 'The Life of Pi' which has subsequently been made into a film?

4) Which two places feature predominantly in the TV comedy series 'Gavin and Stacey'?

5) In the sitcom Only Fools and Horses, what was the name and nickname of the professional criminal who was also Rodney's potential father, and was portrayed by Nicholas Lyndhurst in 'Rock and Chips'?

6) What is the name of Lord Melchett's pigeon in Blackadder Goes Forth?

7) What is the name of the character which features in the Sherlock Holmes stories who is described as 'The Napoleon of crime'?

8) Which famous musician, and his wife, was attacked by an intruder with a knife in his home in Oxfordshire in 1999?

9) In which country was Chris De Burgh born?

10) What is Voldemort's real name in the Harry Potter Books?

(Answers for quiz 149 are below quiz number 1)

Quiz 147 – Answers

1) The Galley, 2) In your fingers and toes, 3) NaCl, 4) Casein, 5) ZXC, 6) Litmus paper, 7) Blood groups, 8) Four times, 9) Universal Serial Bus, 10) Zoology

1) Fill in the missing USSR leader: Lenin, Stalin, Malenkov, [.....], Brezhnev?

2) How many days before Easter Sunday is Ash Wednesday?

3) What was the Roman name for Scotland?

4) What is the name of the street that the White House is situated on?

5) Which country's cars have the international vehicle registration code of the letter 'E'?

6) True or false, in a game of cricket, a batsman can be run out on a no-ball?

7) A semitone is split into 100 intervals of what?

8) Which film character is Richard Kiel famous for playing?

9) Who is said to have 'fiddled' while Rome burnt down?

10) Which 'Spice' was Mel C?

(Answers for quiz 150 are below quiz number 2)

1) Charles Lindbergh, 2) New Musical Express, 3) Colchester, 4) Snowy, 5) Spirit of Ecstasy, 6) Shoes, 7) A used furniture dealer, 8) Eminem, 9) Caves, 10) The Grimm Brothers

Printed in Great Britain
by Amazon

48206805R00090